Objectivity and Liberal Scholarship

Objectivity and Liberal Scholarship

NOAM CHOMSKY

THE NEW PRESS

NEW YORK
LONDON

The excerpts from *Homage to Catalonia* by George Orwell, on pages 70–71,
are reprinted by permission of Harcourt, Brace & World, Inc.
Copyright 1952 by Sonia Brownell Orwell.

The first part of "Objectivity and Liberal Scholarship" is based on a lecture
by the same title originally delivered as part of the Albert Schweitzer Lecture Series
at New York University, which appears in *Power and Consciousness in Society,*
New York University Press, New York. We gratefully acknowledge permission
by the Schweitzer Program in the Humanities to use this work.

This essay, "Objectivity and Liberal Scholarship," was first published as part of
American Power and the New Mandarins, by Pantheon Books,
a division of Random House, Inc., New York, 1969
This edition published by The New Press, New York, 2003
Distributed by W. W. Norton & Company, Inc., New York

ISBN 1-56584-858-6 (pbk.)
CIP data available

The New Press was established in 1990 as a not-for-profit alternative to the large,
commercial publishing houses currently dominating the book publishing industry.
The New Press operates in the public interest rather than for private gain, and is committed
to publishing, in innovative ways, works of educational, cultural, and community value
that are often deemed insufficiently profitable.

The New Press, 38 Greene Street, 4th floor, New York, NY 10013
www.thenewpress.com

In the United Kingdom: 6 Salem Road, London W2 4BU

Composition by dix!

Printed in Canada

2   4   6   8   10   9   7   5   3   1

Foreword
by Martin Duberman[*]

There is no shortage these days of critiques of American power, but Chomsky's formulation is quite special, and his tone—so free of exaggeration or misrepresentation—is all but unique. He avoids self-righteousness ("No one," he writes in a characteristic passage, "who involved himself in anti-war ac-tivities as late as 1965, as I did, has any reason for pride or sat-

when the evidence allows for several possible conclusions; and is able to see inadequacies in the views or tactics of those who share his position—and even some occasional merit in those who do not. These qualities—this integrity—gives unusual strength to Chomsky's writing.

Unlike many radical critics, Chomsky does not build his case against our country's foreign policy by magnifying the innocence or goodness of those who oppose us internationally. He argues brilliantly against the official American view that our interventionist policies are merely a defensive reaction to Russian or Chinese aggression, that we intervene only

[*] The author is Distinguished Professor of History at City University of New York, and the author of some twenty books, including *Paul Robeson: A Biography* (The New Press). His most recent is the forthcoming novel *Haymarket*. He is currently at work on the authorized biography of Lincoln Kirstein.

to defend the people of Asia (or Africa, or Latin-America) from the horrors of totalitarianism. At the same time he declares that "one may still react with dismay, perhaps even outrage, to the authoritarian and repressive character of the Chinese state," and refers to the former Soviet Union as "consolidating its Eastern European empire with brutality and deceit." He knows that the case against our imperialist ventures is so strong that it does not require the varnishing of our "antagonists" for its force.

A corollary of not finding an anti-American stance automatically self-purifying is the ability to find something of value still adhering to our own society. Chomsky is reluctant to put much emphasis on the positive aspects of our culture—understandably, since the central aim of his book is to make us aware of how destructive our self-infatuation has become. Yet he does remind us in passing that free institutions, however compromised by passivity and conformity, continue to exist, that "it is to the great credit of the American press," for example, that "it does still provide information on the basis of which one who is willing to put in the time and effort can arrive at some understanding of what is taking place" (though few, he adds, have the patience to absorb that information—or, for that matter, the slogan-free perspective from which to evaluate it).

Even as regards the peace movement, of which he himself has been so important a figure, Chomsky avoids a one-dimensional evaluation; indeed, he is more critical than congratulatory. We have reached the peace table at Paris, he argues, not because the peace movement has produced a fundamental change of heart about our country's right to intervene in the internal affairs of other nations, but simply because the public has come to feel that our involvement is costing too much. I have some peripheral doubts about this interpretation: "cost," at least, must be defined to include not merely such things as a tax surcharge, but also the rise in casualty lists and draft calls; moreover, I think some segment of public opinion, particularly in campus communities, has moved beyond cost accounting arguments into an opposition based on ethical considerations.

In any case, Chomsky is surely right that opposition to the Vietnam War has chiefly resulted from the war's lack of success. Even "enlightened" American opinion still accepts our right to intervene abroad so long as we do so expeditiously. Chomsky holds the peace movement itself at least partly responsible for the public's failure to disavow our *right* to intervene. One could argue that Chomsky mistakenly equates the peace movement's failure to produce fundamental results with an unwillingness to try for them, or that he underestimates the change that *has* taken place in public opinion. Even some "liberal mandarins," it might be said, have come to understand that the central question is our right, not merely our ability, to intervene. But the basic facts remain as Chomsky states them: most opponents of the war in Vietnam thought Johnson was a usurper and Vietnam an aberration; *ordinarily,* they argued, we do not interfere with the affairs of other nations—or when we do, it is only because *someone* must dictate "acceptable" patterns of social organization.

Along with the even-handedness of his analysis, Chomsky seems to me remarkable among our radical critics for at least one other quality: whereas many of those critics (and especially the older ones) do not recognize the anarchist perspective that lies at the heart of the rebellion of the young, Chomsky not only recognizes, but admires it. He calls "the revival of anarchist thinking . . . and the attempts to put it into effect . . . the most promising development of the past years," a development which allows him to conclude, even after detailing the horrors of American power, that "there now exist opportunities for change that are not very likely to recur."

Chomsky's appreciation of the anti-authoritarian, "participatory" aspects of anarchism is based on historical as well as con-

temporary material. In a detailed examination of the Spanish
Civil War, he points to the failure of almost all those who have
written on it to acknowledge the importance of the anarchists.
At the heart of "Objectivity and Liberal Scholarship" is an eru-
dite, lucid rebuttal of the view of the Spanish Civil War dominant
among historians (for which read "liberal intellectuals"): that
"Communist policy was in essentials the correct one—that in
order to consolidate domestic and international support for the
Republic it was necessary to block and then reverse the social
revolution." The revolution to which Chomsky refers, largely
unplanned, inarticulate and unrecorded, centered in the masses
of urban and rural laborers and was in spirit predominantly anar-
chistic. Liberal (and Communist) historians have never given due
recognition to that revolution because—despite their claims to
objectivity—they have a built-in bias against mass movements,
the dispossessed, and all that bears the mark of spontaneity or
loose organization. As a result, historians of the Spanish Civil War
have ignored some of its crucial aspects or have underplayed
them as naïve, primitive and irrational—as fringe developments.

I think Chomsky makes his case about the Spanish Civil War,
and in doing so raises a critical issue about historical scholarship.
By showing that our scholars judge historical evidence according to their own elitist, rationalist, "orderly" assumptions, and
thereby distort that evidence, Chomsky makes us aware of how
much our understanding of the world is predicated on a desper-
ately one-sided view of its history.

I think he overstates the extent to which mandarin assumptions ("opposition to social change and support for the counterrevolutionary violence that is used to suppress it") have *always*
characterized our cultural history. He cites for proof a book by
Louis Hartz, a historian known for emphasizing continuity and
consensus (as opposed to change and conflict) in our past—one
of those very liberals, in other words, whom Chomsky otherwise

warns us against. At any rate, Chomsky makes his point that in his generation at least, liberal intellectuals have done much to encourage the view now so common in our country (especially among the "well-educated") that the masses are "objects, incapable of political expression or allegiance, to be 'controlled' by one side or the other." Chomsky might take some heart from knowing that a new generation of academics has begun to repair the damages wrought by liberal scholarship. Utilizing neglected sources and seeing traditional sources with new eyes, radical historians are these days exploring far more the "inarticulate impulses" of the masses.

I've commented on only two or three of the more significant aspects of Chomsky's remarkable book; but its riches cannot so easily be exhausted. One of the few comforts available at this terrible moment is that we continue to produce men of Noam Chomsky's honesty and stature—and continue to have them published.

This is a slightly edited version of Mr. Duberman's review of Noam Chomsky's American Power and the New Mandarins *(in which "Objectivity and Liberal Scholarship" is the lead essay). It appeared in* The New Republic *on April 19, 1969, p. 27. Reprinted with permission.*

Objectivity and Liberal Scholarship

I

In a recent essay, Conor Cruise O'Brien speaks of the process of "counterrevolutionary subordination" which poses a threat to scholarly integrity in our own counterrevolutionary society, just as "revolutionary subordination," a phenomenon often noted and rightly deplored, has undermined scholarly integrity in revolutionary and postrevolutionary situations.[1] He observes that "power in our time has more intelligence in its service, and allows that intelligence more discretion as to its methods, than ever before in history," and suggests that this development is not altogether encouraging, since we have moved perceptibly towards the state of "a society maimed through the systematic corruption of its intelligence." He urges that "increased and specific vigilance, not just the elaboration of general principles, is required from the intellectual community toward specific growing dangers to its integrity."

Senator Fulbright has developed a similar theme in an important and perceptive speech.[2] He describes the failure of the uni-

Parts of this essay were delivered as a lecture at New York University in March 1968, as part of the Albert Schweitzer Lecture Series, and appeared in *Power and Consciousness in Society,* edited by Conor Cruise O'Brien and published by New York University Press. I am indebted to Paul Potter, André Schiffrin, and William Watson for very helpful comments.

versities to form "an effective counterweight to the military-industrial complex by strengthening their emphasis on the traditional values of our democracy." Instead they have "joined the monolith, adding greatly to its power and influence." Specifically, he refers to the failure of the social scientists, "who ought to be acting as responsible and independent critics of the Government's policies," but who instead become the agents of these policies. "While young dissenters plead for resurrection of the American promise, their elders continue to subvert it." With "the surrender of independence, the neglect of teaching, and the distortion of scholarship," the university "is not only failing to meet its responsibilities to its students; it is betraying a public trust."

The extent of this betrayal might be argued; its existence, as a threatening tendency, is hardly in doubt! Senator Fulbright mentions one primary cause: the access to money and influence. Others might be mentioned: for example, a highly restrictive, almost universally shared ideology, and the inherent dynamics of professionalization. As to the former, Fulbright has cited elsewhere the observation of De Tocqueville: "I know of no country in which there is so little independence of mind and real freedom of discussion as in America." Free institutions certainly exist, but a tradition of passivity and conformism restricts their use—the cynic might say this is why they continue to exist. The impact of professionalization is also quite clear. The "free-floating intellectual" may occupy himself with problems because of their inherent interest and importance, perhaps to little effect. The professional, however, tends to define his problems on the basis of the technique that he has mastered, and has a natural desire to apply his skills. Commenting on this process, Senator Clark quotes the remarks of Dr. Harold Agnew, director of the Los Alamos Laboratories Weapons Division: "The basis of advanced technology is innovation and nothing is more stifling to innovation than seeing one's product not used or ruled out of consideration on flimsy premises involving public world opinion"[3] —"a shocking statement and a dangerous one," as Clark rightly comments. In much the same way, behavioral scientists who believe themselves to be in possession of certain techniques of control and manipulation will tend to search for problems to which their knowledge and skills might be relevant, defining these as the "important problems"; and it will come as no surprise that they occasionally express their contempt for "flimsy premises involving public world opinion" that restrict the application of these skills. Thus among engineers, there are the "weapons cultists" who construct their bombs and missiles, and among the behavioral scientists, we find the technicians who design and carry out "experiments with population and resources control methods" in Vietnam.[4]

These various factors—access to power, shared ideology, professionalization—may or may not be deplorable in themselves, but there can be no doubt that they interact so as to pose a serious threat to the integrity of scholarship in fields that are struggling for intellectual content and are thus particularly susceptible to the workings of a kind of Gresham's law. What is more, the subversion of scholarship poses a threat to society at large. The danger is particularly great in a society that encourages specialization and stands in awe of technical expertise. In such circumstances, the opportunities are great for the abuse of knowledge and technique—to be more exact, the claim to knowledge and technique. Taking note of these dangers, one reads with concern the claims of some social scientists that their discipline is essential for the training of those to whom they refer as "the mandarins of the future."[5] Philosophy and literature still "have their value," so Ithiel Pool informs us, but it is psychology, sociology, systems analysis, and political science that provide the knowledge by which "men of power are humanized and civilized." In no small

measure, the Vietnam war was designed and executed by these
new mandarins, and it testifies to the concept of humanity and
civilization they are likely to bring to the exercise of power.[6]

Is the new access to power of the technical intelligentsia a
delusion or a growing reality? There are those who perceive the
"skeletal structure of a new society" in which the leadership will
rest "with the research corporation, the industrial laboratories,
the experimental stations, and the universities," with "the scientists, the mathematicians, the economists, and the engineers of
the new computer technology"—"not only the best talents, but
eventually the entire complex of social prestige and social status,
will be rooted in the intellectual and scientific communities."[7] A
careful look at the "skeletal structure" of this new society, if such
it is, is hardly reassuring. As Daniel Bell points out, "it has been
war rather than peace that has been largely responsible for the ac-
ceptance of planning and technocratic modes in government,"
and our present "mobilized society" is one that is geared to the
"social goal" of "military and war preparedness." Bell's relative
optimism regarding the new society comes from his assumption
that the university is "the place where theoretical knowledge is
sought, tested, and codified in a disinterested way" and that "the
mobilized postures of the Cold War and the space race" are a
temporary aberration, a reaction to Communist aggressiveness.
In contrast, a strong argument can be made that the university
has, to a significant degree, betrayed its public trust; that matters
of foreign policy are very much "a reflex of internal political
forces" as well as of economic institutions (rather than "a judgment about the national interest, involving strategy decisions
based on the calculations of an opponent's strength and inten-
tions"); that the mobilization for war is not "irony" but a natural
development, given our present social and economic organization; that the technologists who achieve power are those who
can perform a service for existing institutions; and that nothing

but catastrophe is to be expected from still further centralization of decision making in government and a narrowing base of corporate affiliates. The experience of the past few years gives little reason to feel optimistic about these developments.

Quite generally, what grounds are there for supposing that those whose claim to power is based on knowledge and technique will be more benign in their exercise of power than those whose claim is based on wealth or aristocratic origin? On the contrary, one might expect the new mandarin to be dangerously arrogant, aggressive, and incapable of adjusting to failure, as compared with his predecessor, whose claim to power was not diminished by honesty as to the limitations of his knowledge, lack of work to do, or demonstrable mistakes.[8] In the Vietnam catastrophe, all of these factors are detectable. There is no point in overgeneralizing, but neither history nor psychology nor sociology gives us any particular reason to look forward with hope to the rule of the new mandarins.

In general, one would expect any group with access to power and affluence to construct an ideology that will justify this state of affairs on grounds of the general welfare. For just this reason, Bell's thesis that intellectuals are moving closer to the center of power, or at least being absorbed more fully into the decision-making structure, is to some extent supported by the phenomenon of counterrevolutionary subordination noted earlier. That is, one might anticipate that as power becomes more accessible, the inequities of the society will recede from vision, the status quo will seem less flawed, and the preservation of order will become a matter of transcendent importance. The fact is that American intellectuals are increasingly achieving the status of a doubly privileged elite: first, as American citizens, with respect to the rest of the world; and second, because of their role in American society, which is surely quite central, whether or not Bell's prediction proves accurate. In such a situation, the dangers of counterrevolutionary subordination, in both the domestic and the international arena, are apparent. I think that O'Brien is entirely correct in pointing to the necessity for "increased and specific vigilance" towards the danger of counterrevolutionary subordination, of which, as he correctly remarks, "we hear almost nothing." I would like to devote this essay to a number of examples.

Several years ago it was enthusiastically proclaimed that "the fundamental political problems of the industrial revolution have been solved," and that "this very triumph of democratic social evolution in the West ends domestic politics for those intellectuals who must have ideologies or utopias to motivate them to social action." [9] During this period of faith in "the end of ideology," even enlightened and informed commentators were inclined to present the most remarkable evaluations of the state of American society. Daniel Bell, for example, wrote that "in the mass consumption economy all groups can easily acquire the outward badges of status and erase the visible demarcations." [10] Writing in *Commentary* in October 1964, he maintained that we have in effect already achieved "the egalitarian and socially mobile society which the 'free floating intellectuals' associated with the Marxist tradition have been calling for during the last hundred years." Granting the obvious general rise in standard of living, the judgment of Gunnar Myrdal seems far more appropriate to the actual situation when he says: "The common idea that America is an immensely rich and affluent country is very much an exaggeration. American affluence is heavily mortgaged. America carries a tremendous burden of debt to its poor people. That this debt must be paid is not only a wish of the do-gooders. Not paying it implies a risk for the social order and for democracy as we have known it." [11] Surely the claim that *all* groups can easily enter the mass-consumption economy and "erase the visible demarcations" is a considerable exaggeration. Similar evaluations of American society appear frequently in contemporary scholarship. To mention just one example, consider the analysis that Adam Ulam gives of Marx's concept of capitalism: "One cannot blame a contemporary observer like Marx for his conviction that industrial fanaticism and self-righteousness were indelible traits of the capitalist. That the capitalist would grow more humane, that he would slacken in his ceaseless pursuit of accumulation and expansion, were not impressions readily warranted by the English social scene of the 1840's and '50's."[12] Again, granting the important changes in industrial society over the past century, it still comes as a surprise to hear that the capitalist has slackened in his ceaseless pursuit of accumulation and expansion.[13]

Remarks such as these illustrate a failure to come to grips with the reality of contemporary society which may not be directly traceable to the newly found (or at least hopefully sought) access to power and affluence, but which is, nevertheless, what one would expect in the developing ideology of a new privileged elite.

Various strands of this ideology are drawn together in a recent article by Zbigniew Brzezinski,[14] in which a number of the conceptions and attitudes that appear in recent social thought are summarized—I am tempted to say "parodied." Brzezinski too sees a "profound change" taking place in the intellectual community, as "the largely humanist-oriented, occasionally ideologically-minded intellectual-dissenter, who sees his role largely in terms of proffering social critiques, is rapidly being displaced either by experts and specialists, who become involved in special governmental undertakings, or by the generalists-integrators, who become in effect house-ideologues for those in power, pro-

viding overall intellectual integration for disparate actions." He
suggests that these "organisation-oriented, application-minded
intellectuals" can be expected to introduce broader and more relevant concerns into the political system—though there is, as he
notes, a danger that "intellectual detachment and the disinterested search for truth" will come to an end, given the new access
of the "application-minded intellectuals" to "power, prestige, and
the good life." They are a new meritocratic elite, "taking over
American life, utilising the universities, exploiting the latest techniques of communications, harnessing as rapidly as possible the
most recent technological devices." Presumably, their civilizing
impact is revealed by the great progress that has been made, in
this new "historical era" that America alone has already entered,
with respect to the problems that confounded the bumbling political leaders of past eras—the problems of the cities, of pollu-
tion, of waste and destructiveness, of exploitation and poverty.
Under the leadership of this "new breed of politicians-
intellectuals," America has become "*the* creative society; the others, consciously and unconsciously, are emulative." We see this,
for example, in mathematics, the biological sciences, anthropol-
ogy, philosophy, cinema, music, historical scholarship, and so on,
where other cultures, hopelessly outdistanced, merely observe
and imitate what America creates. Thus we move towards a new
world-wide " 'super-culture,' strongly influenced by American
life, with its own universal electronic-computer language," with
an enormous and growing "psycho-cultural gap" separating
America from the rest of the "developed world."

It is impossible even to imagine what Brzezinski thinks a "universal electronic-computer language" may be, or what cultural
values he thinks will be created by the new "technologically
dominant and conditioned technetron" who, he apparently believes, may prove to be the true "repository of that indefinable
quality we call human." It would hardly be rewarding to try to

disentangle Brzezinski's confusions and misunderstandings. What is interesting, rather, is the way his dim awareness of current developments in science and technology is used to provide an ideological justification for the "increasing role in the key decision-making institutions of individuals with special intellectual and scientific attainments," the new "organisation-oriented, application-minded intellectuals" based in the university, "the creative eye of the massive communications complex."

Parallel to the assumption that all is basically well at home is the widely articulated belief that the problems of international society, too, would be subject to intelligent management were it not for the machinations of the Communists. One aspect of this complacence is the belief that the Cold War was entirely the result of Russian (later Chinese) aggressiveness. For example, Daniel Bell has described the origins of the Cold War in the following terms: "When the Russians began stirring up the Greek guerrilla EAM in what had been tacitly acknowledged at Teheran as a British sphere of influence, the Communists began their cry against Anglo-American imperialism. Following the rejection of the Marshall Plan and the Communist coup in Czechoslovakia in February, 1948, the Cold War was on in earnest." [15] Clearly, this will hardly do as a balanced and objective statement of the origins of the Cold War, but the distortion it reflects is an inherent element in Bell's optimism about the new society, since it enables him to maintain that our Cold War posture is purely reactive, and that once Communist belligerence is tamed, the new technical intelligentsia can turn its attention to the construction of a more decent society.

A related element in the ideology of the liberal intellectual is the firm belief in the fundamental generosity of Western policy towards the Third World. Adam Ulam again provides a typical example: "Problems of an international society undergoing an economic and ideological revolution seem to defy . . . the gen-

erosity—granted its qualifications and errors—that has characterized the policy of the leading democratic powers of the
West."[16] Even Hans Morgenthau succumbs to this illusion. He
summarizes a discussion of intervention with these remarks: "We
have intervened in the political, military and economic affairs of
other countries to the tune of far in excess of $100 billion, and
we are at present involved in a costly and risky war in order to
build a nation in South Vietnam. Only the enemies of the
United States will question the generosity of these efforts, which
have no parallel in history."[17] Whatever one may think about the
$100 billion, it is difficult to see why anyone should take seri-
ously the professed "generosity" of our effort to build a nation in
South Vietnam, any more than the similar professions of benevolence by our many forerunners in such enterprises. Generosity
has never been a commodity in short supply among powers bent
on extending their hegemony.

Still another strand in the ideology of the new emerging elite
is the concern for order, for maintaining the status quo, which is
now seen to be quite favorable and essentially just. An excellent
example is the statement by fourteen leading political scientists
and historians on United States Asian policy, recently distributed
by the Freedom House Public Affairs Institute.[18] These scholars
designate themselves as "the moderate segment of the academic
community." The designation is accurate; they stand midway between the two varieties of extremism, one which demands that
we destroy everyone who stands in our path, the other, that we
adopt the principles of international behavior we require of
every other world power. The purpose of their statement is to
"challenge those among us who, overwhelmed by guilt com-
plexes, find comfort in asserting or implying that we are always
wrong, our critics always right, and that only doom lies ahead."
They find our record in Asia to be "remarkably good," and ap-
plaud our demonstrated ability to rectify mistakes, our "capacity

for pragmatism and self-examination," and our "healthy avoidance of narrow nationalism," capacities which distinguish us "among the major societies of this era."

The moderate scholars warn that "to avoid a major war in the Asia-Pacific region, it is essential that the United States continue to deter, restrain, and counterbalance Chinese power." True, "China has exercised great prudence in avoiding a direct confrontation with the United States or the Soviet Union" since the Korean War, and it is likely that China will "continue to substitute words for acts while concentrating upon domestic issues." Still, we cannot be certain of this and must therefore continue our efforts to tame the dragon. One of the gravest problems posed by China is its policy of "isolationist fanaticism"—obviously, a serious threat to peace. Another danger is the terrifying figure of Mao Tse-tung, a romantic, who refuses to accept the "bureaucratism essential to the ordering of this enormously complex, extremely difficult society." The moderate scholars would feel much more at ease with the familiar sort of technical expert, who is committed to the "triumph of bureaucratism" and who refrains from romantic efforts to undermine the party apparatus and the discipline it imposes.

Furthermore, the moderate scholars announce their support for "our basic position" in Vietnam. A Communist victory in Vietnam, they argue, would "gravely jeopardize the possibilities for a political equilibrium in Asia, seriously damage our credibility, deeply affect the morale—and the policies—of our Asian allies and the neutrals." By a "political equilibrium," they do not, of course, refer to the status quo as of 1945–1946 or as outlined by international agreement at Geneva in 1954. They do not explain why the credibility of the United States is more important than the credibility of the indigenous elements in Vietnam who have dedicated themselves to a war of national liberation. Nor do they explain why the morale of the military dictatorships of Thailand

and Taiwan must be preserved. They merely hint darkly of the dangers of a third world war, dangers which are real enough and which are increased when advocates of revolutionary change face an external counterrevolutionary force. In principle, such dangers can be lessened by damping revolutionary ardor or by withdrawing the counterrevolutionary force. The latter alternative, however, is unthinkable, irresponsible.

The crucial assumption in the program of the moderate scholars is that we must not encourage "those elements committed to the thesis that violence is the best means of effecting change." It is important to recognize that it is not violence as such to which the moderate scholars object. On the contrary, they approve of our violence in Vietnam, which, as they are well aware, enormously exceeds that of the Vietnamese enemy. To further underline this point, they cite as our greatest triumph in Southeast Asia the "dramatic changes" which have taken place in Indonesia—the most dramatic being the massacre of several hundred thousand people. But this massacre, like our extermination of Vietnamese, is not a use of violence to effect social change and is therefore legitimate. What is more, it may be that those massacred were largely ethnic Chinese and landless peasants, and that the "countercoup" in effect re-established traditional authority more firmly.[19] If so, all the more reason why we should not deplore this use of violence; and in fact, the moderate scholars delicately refrain from alluding to it in their discussion of dramatic changes in Indonesia. We must conclude that when these scholars deplore the use of violence to effect change, it is not the violence but rather steps toward social change that they find truly disturbing. Social change that departs from the course we plot is not to be tolerated. The threat to order is too great.

So great is the importance of stability and order that even reform of the sort that receives American authorization must often be delayed, the moderate scholars emphasize. "Indeed, many types of reform increase instability, however desirable and essential they may be in long-range terms. For people under siege, there is no substitute for security." The reference, needless to say, is not to security from American bombardment, but rather to security from the wrong sorts of political and social change.

The policy recommendations of the moderate scholars are based on their particular ideological bias, namely, that a certain form of stability—not that of North Vietnam or North Korea, but that of Thailand, Taiwan, or the Philippines—is so essential that we must be willing to use our unparalleled means of violence to ensure that it is preserved. It is instructive to see how other mentors of the new mandarins describe the problem of order and reform. Ithiel Pool formulates the central issue as follows:

> In the Congo, in Vietnam, in the Dominican Republic, it is clear that order depends on somehow compelling newly mobilized strata to return to a measure of passivity and defeatism from which they have recently been aroused by the process of modernization. At least temporarily, the maintenance of order requires a lowering of newly acquired aspirations and levels of political activity.[20]

This is what "we have learned in the past thirty years of intensive empirical study of contemporary societies." Pool is merely describing facts, not proposing policy. A corresponding version of the facts is familiar on the domestic scene: workers threaten the public order by striking for their demands, the impatience of the Negro community threatens the stability of the body politic. One can, of course, imagine another way in which order can be preserved in all such cases: namely, by meeting the demands, or at the very least by removing the barriers that have been placed, by force which may be latent and disguised, in the way of attempts to satisfy the "newly acquired aspirations." But this might mean that the wealthy and powerful would have to sacrifice some degree of privilege, and it is therefore excluded as a method for maintenance of order. Such proposals are likely to meet with little sympathy from Pool's new mandarins.

From the doubly privileged position of the American scholar, the transcendent importance of order, stability, and nonviolence (by the oppressed) seems entirely obvious: to others, the matter is not so simple. If we listen, we hear such voices as this, from an economist in India:

> It is disingenuous to invoke "democracy," "due process of law," "non-violence," to rationalise the absence of action. For meaningful concepts under such conditions become meaningless since, in reality, they justify the relentless pervasive exploitation of the masses; at once a denial of democracy and a more sinister form of violence perpetrated on the overwhelming majority through contractual forms.[21]

Moderate American scholarship does not seem capable of comprehending these simple truths.

It would be wrong to leave the impression that the ideology of the liberal intelligentsia translates itself into policy as a rain of cluster bombs and napalm. In fact, the liberal experts have been dismayed by the emphasis on military means in Vietnam and have consistently argued that the key to our efforts should be social restructuring and economic assistance. Correspondingly, I think that we can perceive more clearly the attitudes that are crystallizing among the new mandarins by considering the technical studies of pacification, for example, the research monograph of William Nighswonger, cited earlier (see note 4). The author, now a professor of political science, was senior United States civilian representative of the Agency for International Development in Quang Nam Province from 1962 to 1964. As he sees the situation, "the knotty problems of pacification are intricately intertwined with the issues of political development and they necessitate—at this time in history—intimate American involvement." Thus Americans must ask some "basic questions of value and obligation—questions that transcend the easy legalisms of 'self-determination' and 'nonintervention.' " These easy legalisms have little relevance to a world in which the West is challenged by "the sophisticated methodology and quasi-religious motivation of Communist insurgency." It is our duty, in the interest of democracy and freedom, to apply our expertise to these twin goals: "to isolate the enemy and destroy his influence and control over the rural population, and to win the peasant's willing support through effective local administration and programs of rural improvement." "An underlying assumption is that insurgency ought to be defeated—for the sake of human rights. . . ." Despite the "remarkable achievements in economic and social development" in Russia and China, "The South Vietnamese peasant deserves something better," and we must give it to him—as we have in Latin America and the Philippines—even if this requires abandoning the easy legalisms of the past and intervening with military force.

Of course, it won't be easy. The enemy has enormous advantages. For one thing, "as in China, the insurgents in Vietnam have exploited the Confucian tenets of ethical rule both by their attacks on government corruption and by exemplary Communist behavior"; and "the Viet-Cong inherited, after Geneva, much of the popular support and sympathies previously attached to the Viet-Minh in the South." After the fall of Diem, matters became still worse: ". . . vast regions that had been under government control quickly came under the influence of the Viet-Cong." By late 1964 the pacification of Quang Nam Province had become "all but impossible," and the worst of it is that "the battle for

Quang Nam was lost by the government to Viet-Cong forces recruited for the most part from within the province." [22] By 1966,
the Vietcong seem so well entrenched in rural areas that "only a
highly imaginative and comprehensive counterinsurgency campaign, with nearly perfect execution and substantial military support, would be capable of dislodging such a powerful and
extensive insurgent apparatus."

A major difficulty we face is the "progressive social and economic results" shown by the Vietcong efforts. An AID report in
March 1965 explains the problem. Comparing "our 'new life
hamlets' " to the Vietcong hamlets, the report comments as follows:

> The basic differences are that the VC hamlets are well organized,
> clean, economically self supporting and have an active defense
> system. For example, a cottage industry in one hamlet was as large
> as has been previously witnessed anywhere in Chuong Thien
> province. New canals are being dug and pineapples are under cul-
> tivation. The VC also have a relocation program for younger
> families. These areas coincide with the areas just outside the
> planned GVN sphere of interest. Unless the USOM/GVN activ-
> ities exhibit a more qualitative basis [sic], there is little likelihood
> of changing the present attitudes of the people. For example, in
> one area only five kilometers from the province capital, the peo-
> ple refused medical assistance offered by ARVN medics.

However, all is not lost. Even though "the Viet-Cong strength in
the countryside has made a 'quantum leap' from its position of
early 1962," there is a compensating factor, namely, "the coun-
terinsurgent military capability was revolutionized by substantial
American troop inputs." This allows us entirely new options. For
example, we can implement more effectively some of the "experiments with population and resources control methods" that
were tried by the USOM and the National Police as early as

1961, though with little success. Given the new possibilities for "material and human resources control," we may even recapture some of the population—a serious matter: "Given the enormous numbers of South Vietnamese citizens presently allied with the Viet-Cong (for whatever reason), the recovery of these peasants for the national cause must be made one of the central tasks of the pacification enterprise."

If we are going to succeed in implementing "material and human resources control," we must moderate ARVN behavior somehow. Thus, according to an AID report of February 1965, "A high incident rate of stealing, robbing, raping and obtaining free meals in the rural areas has not endeared the population towards ARVN or Regional Forces." Nor did it improve matters when many civilians witnessed a case in which an ARVN company leader killed a draft dodger, disemboweled him, "took his heart and liver out and had them cooked at a restaurant," after which "the heart and liver were eaten by a number of soldiers." Such acts cause great difficulties, especially in trying to combat an enemy so vile as to practice "exemplary Communist behavior."

More generally, "the success of pacification requires that there be survivors to be pacified," and given "the sheer magnitude of American, Korean, Australian and indigenous Vietnamese forces," which has so severely "strained the economic and social equilibrium of the nation," it is sometimes difficult to ensure this minimal condition.

There are other problems, for example, "the difficulty of denying food to the enemy" in the Mekong Delta; "the hunger for land ownership," which, for some curious reason, is never satisfied by our friends in Saigon; the corruption; occasional bombing of the "wrong" village; the pervasive "Viet-Cong infiltration of military and civilian government organization"; the fact that when we relocate peasants to new hamlets, we often leave "the fox still in the henhouse," because of inadequate police methods; and so on.

Still, we have a good "pacification theory," which involves three steps: "elimination of the Viet-Cong by search-and-destroy operations, protection and control of the population and its resources by police and military forces, and preparing and arming the peasants to defend their own communities." If we rarely reach the third stage, this is because we have not yet learned to "share the sense of urgency of the revolutionary cause," or "to nourish these attitudes" among our "Vietnamese associates." Thus *we* understand that the "real revolution" is the one we are implementing, "in contrast to the artificially stimulated and controlled revolution of Diem and the Communists," but we have difficulties in communicating this fact to the Vietnamese peasant or to our "Vietnamese associates." What is needed, clearly, is better training for American officials, and of course, true national dedication to this humanitarian task.

A grave defect in our society, this political scientist argues, is our tendency to avoid "an active American role in the fostering of democratic institutions abroad." The pacification program in Vietnam represents an attempt to meet our responsibility to foster democratic institutions abroad, through rational methods of material and human resources control. Refusal to dedicate ourselves to this task might be described as "a policy more selfish and timid than it was broad and enlightened,"[23] to use the terminology of an earlier day.

When we strip away the terminology of the behavioral sciences, we see revealed, in such work as this, the mentality of the colonial civil servant, persuaded of the benevolence of the mother country and the correctness of its vision of world order, and convinced that he understands the true interests of the backward peoples whose welfare he is to administer. In fact, much of the scholarly work on Southeast Asian affairs reflects precisely this mentality. As an example, consider the August 1967 issue of *Asian Survey*, fully devoted to a Vietnam symposium in which a number of experts contribute their thoughts on the success of our enterprise and how it can be moved forward. The introductory essay by Samuel Huntington, chairman of the department of government at Harvard, is entitled "Social Science and Vietnam." It emphasizes the need "to develop scholarly study and understanding of Vietnam" if our "involvement" is to succeed, and expresses his judgment that the papers in this volume "demonstrate that issues and topics closely connected to policy can be presented and analyzed in scholarly and objective fashion."

Huntington's own contribution to "scholarly study and understanding of Vietnam" includes an article in the *Boston Globe*, February 17, 1968. Here he describes the "momentous changes in Vietnamese society during the past five years," specifically, the process of urbanization. This process "struck directly at the strength and potential appeal of the Viet Cong." "So long as the overwhelming mass of the people lived in the countryside, the VC could win the war by winning control of those people—and they came very close to doing so in both 1961 and 1964. But the American sponsored urban revolution undercut the VC rural revolution." The refugees fleeing from the rural areas found not only security but also "prosperity and economic well-being." "While wartime urban prosperity hurt some, the mass of the poor people benefited from it."

The sources of urbanization have been described clearly many times, for example, by this American spokesman in Vietnam: "There have been three choices open to the peasantry. One, to stay where they are; two, to move into the areas controlled by us; three, to move off into the interior towards the Vietcong. . . . Our operations have been designed to make the first choice impossible, the second attractive, and to reduce the likelihood of

anyone choosing the third to zero."[24] The benefits accruing to
the newly urbanized elements have also been amply described in
the press, for example, by James Doyle of the *Globe,* February 22,
1968: Saigon "is a rich city, the bar owners, B-girls, money
changers and black marketeers all making their fortunes while it
lasts. It is a poor city, with hundreds of thousands of refugees
crammed into thatched huts and tinroofed shacks, more than two
million people shoehorned into 21 square miles." Or Neil Shee-
han, in a classic and often-quoted article (*New York Times,* October 9, 1966):

> A drive through Saigon demonstrates another fashion in which
> the social system works. Virtually all the new construction con-
> sists of luxury apartments, hotels and office buildings financed by
> Chinese businessmen or affluent Vietnamese with relatives or
> connections within the regime. The buildings are destined to be
> rented to Americans. Saigon's workers live, as they always have, in
> fetid slums on the city's outskirts. . . . Bars and bordellos, thou-
> sands of young Vietnamese·women degrading themselves as bar
> girls and prostitutes, gangs of hoodlums and beggars and children
> selling their older sisters and picking pockets have become ubiq-
> uitous features of urban life.

Many have remarked on the striking difference between the way
in which the press and the visiting scholar describe what they see
in Vietnam. It should occasion no surprise. Each is pursuing his
own craft. The reporter's job is to describe what he sees before
his eyes; many have done so with courage and even brilliance.
The colonial administrator, on the other hand, is concerned to
justify what he has done and what he hopes to do, and—if an
"expert" as well—to construct an appropriate ideological cover,
to show that we are just and righteous in what we do, and to put
nagging doubts to rest. One sees moral degradation and fetid
slums; the other, prosperity and well-being—and if kindly old

Uncle Sam occasionally flicks his ashes on someone by mistake, that is surely no reason for tantrums.

Returning to the collection of scholarly and objective studies in *Asian Survey,* the first, by Kenneth Young, president of the Asia Society, describes our difficulties in "transferring innovations and institutions to the Vietnamese" and calls for the assistance of social scientists in overcoming these difficulties. Social scientists should, he feels, study "the intricacies that effectively inhibit or transfer what the Americans, either by government policy or by the technician's action, want to introduce into the mind of a Vietnamese or into a Vietnamese organization." The problem, in short, is one of communication. For this objective scholar, there is no question of our right to "transfer innovations and institutions to the Vietnamese," by force if necessary, or of our superior insight into the needed innovations or appropriate institutions. In just the same way, Lord Cornwallis understood the necessity of "transferring the institution" of a squirearchy to India—as any reasonable person could see, this was the only civilized form of social organization.

The "scholarly objectivity" that Huntington lauds is further demonstrated in the contribution by Milton Sacks, entitled "Restructuring Government in South Vietnam." As Sacks perceives the situation, there are two forces in South Vietnam, the "nationalists" and the "Communists." The "Communists" are the Vietminh and the NLF; among the "nationalists," he mentions specifically the VNQDD and the Dai Viet (and the military). The "nationalists" have a few problems; for example, they "were manipulated by the French, by the Japanese, by the communists and latterly by the Americans," and "too many of South Vietnam's leading generals fought with the French against the Vietnamese people."[25] Our problem is the weakness of the nationalists, although there was some hope during General Khanh's government, "a most interesting effort because it was a genuine coalition of representatives of all the major political groups in South Vietnam." Curiously, this highly representative government was unable to accept or even to consider "a proposal for what appeared to be an authentic coalition government" coming from the National Liberation Front in mid-1964.[26] According to Douglas Pike, the proposal could not be seriously considered because none of the "non-Communists" in South Vietnam, "with the possible exception of the Buddhists, thought themselves equal in size and power to risk entering into a coalition, fearing that if they did the whale would swallow the minnow." Thus, he continues, "coalition government with a strong NLF could not be sold within South Vietnam," even to the government which, as Sacks informs us, was "a genuine coalition" of "all the major political groups in South Vietnam." Rather, the GVN and its successors continued to insist that the NLF show their sincerity by withdrawing "their armed units and their political cadres from South Vietnamese territory" (March 1, 1965).

According to Sacks, "the problem which presents itself is to devise an institutional arrangement that will tend to counteract the factors and forces which are conducive to that instability" that now plagues Vietnamese political life. This problem, of course, is one that presents itself to *us*. And, Sacks feels, it is well on its way to solution, with the new constitution and the forthcoming (September 1967) elections, which "will provide spokesmen who claim legitimacy through popular mandate and speak with authority on the issues of war and peace for their constituency." Although this "free election . . . will still leave unrepresented those who are fighting under the banner of the South Vietnam National Liberation Front and those whose candidates were not permitted to stand in the elections," we must, after all, understand that no institution in the real world can be perfect. The important thing, according to Sacks, is that for the first time since the fall of Diem, there will be elections that are not seen by the government in power simply "as a means of legitimating the power they already had, using the governmental machinery to underwrite themselves." Putting aside the remarkable naiveté regarding the forthcoming elections, what is striking is the implicit assumption that we have a right to continue our efforts to restructure the South Vietnamese government, in the interests of what we determine to be Vietnamese nationalism. In just the same way, the officers of the Kwantung Army sought to support "genuine Manchurian nationalism," thirty-five years ago.

To understand more fully what is implied by the judgment that we must defend the "nationalists" against the "Communists," we can turn again to Pike's interesting study. The nationalist groups mentioned by Sacks are the VNQDD and the Dai Viet. The former, after its virtual destruction by the French, was revived by the Chinese Nationalists in 1942. "It supported itself through banditry. It executed traitors with a great deal of publicity, and its violent acts in general were carefully conceived for their psychological value." Returning to Vietnam "with the occupying Chinese forces following World War II," it "was of some importance until mid-1946, when it was purged by the Vietminh." "The VNQDD never was a mass political party in the Western sense. At its peak of influence it numbered, by estimates of its own leaders, less than 1,500 persons. Nor was it ever particularly strong in either Central or South Vietnam. It had no formal structure and held no conventions or assemblies." As to the Dai Viet, "Dai Viet membership included leading Vietnamese figures and governmental officials who viewed Japan as a suitable model for Vietnam [N. B. fascist Japan]. The organization never made any particular obeisance either to democracy or to the rank-and-file Vietnamese. It probably never numbered more than 1,000 members and did not consider itself a mass-based organization. It turned away from Western liberalism, although its economic orientation was basically socialist, in favor of authoritarianism and blind obedience." During World War II, "it was at all times strongly pro-Japanese."

In contrast to these genuine nationalists, we have the Vietminh, whose "war was anticolonial, clearly nationalistic, and concerned *all* Vietnamese," and the NLF, which regarded the rural Vietnamese not "simply as a pawn in a power struggle but as the active element in the thrust," which "maintained that its contest with the GVN and the United States should be fought out at a political level and that the use of massed military might was in itself illegitimate," until forced by the Americans and the GVN "to use counterforce to survive." In its internal documents as well as its public pronouncements the NLF insisted, from its earliest days, that its goal must be to "set up a democratic national coalition administration in South Vietnam; realize independence, democratic freedoms, and improvement of the people's living conditions; safeguard peace; and achieve national reunification on the basis of independence and democracy." "Aside from the NLF there has never been a truly mass-based political party in South Vietnam." It organized "the rural population through the instrument of self-control—victory by means of the organizational weapon," setting up a variety of self-help "functional liberation associations" based on "associational discipline" coupled with "the right of freedom of discussion and secret vote at association meetings," and generating "a sense of community, first, by developing a pattern of political thought and behavior appropriate to the social problems of the rural Vietnamese village in the midst of sharp social change and, second, by providing a basis for group action that allowed the individual villager to see that his own efforts could have meaning and effect" (obviously, a skilled and treacherous enemy). This was, of course, prior to "the advent of massive American aid, and the GVN's strategic hamlet program." With the American takeover of the war, the emphasis shifted to military rather than political action, and ultimately, North Vietnamese involvement and perhaps control; "beginning in 1965, large numbers of regular army troops from North Vietnam were sent into South Vietnam."

In short, what we see is a contrast between the Dai Viet and VNQDD, representing South Vietnamese nationalism, and the NLF, an extrinsic alien force. One must bear in mind that Sacks would undoubtedly accept Pike's factual description as accurate, but, like Pike, would regard it as demonstrating nothing, since we are the ultimate arbiters of what counts as "genuine Vietnamese nationalism."

An interesting counterpoint to Sacks's exposition of nationalist versus Communist forces is provided in David Wurfel's careful analysis, in the same issue of *Asian Survey,* of the "Saigon political elite." He argues that "this elite has not substantially changed its character in the last few years" (i.e., since 1962), though there may be a few modifications: "Formerly, only among the great landlords were there those who held significant amounts of both political and economic power; grandiose corruption may have allowed others to attain that distinction in recent years." Continuing, "the military men in post-Diem cabinets all served under Bao Dai and the French in a civil or military capacity." Under the French, "those who felt most comfortable about entering the civil service were those whose families were already part of the bureaucratic-intellectual elite. By the early 1950's they saw radicalism, in the form of the Viet Minh, as a threat to their own position. The present political elite is the legacy of these developments." Although, he observes, things might change, "the South Vietnamese cabinets and perhaps most of the rest of the political elite have been constituted by a highly westernized intelligentsia. Though the people of South Vietnam seem to be in a revolutionary mood, this elite is hardly revolutionary." The NLF con-

stitutes a "counter-elite," less Westernized: of the NLF Central
Committee members, "only 3 out of 27 report studying in
France."

The problem of "restructuring government" is further analyzed by Ithiel Pool, along lines that parallel Sack's contribution
to this collection of "scholarly, objective studies." He begins by
formulating a general proposition: "I rule out of consideration
here a large range of viable political settlements," namely, those
that involve "the inclusion of the Viet Cong in a coalition government or even the persistence of the Viet Cong as a legal organization in South Vietnam." Such arrangements "are not
acceptable"—to us, that is. The only acceptable settlement is one
"imposed by the GVN despite the persisting great political
power of the Viet Cong."

There is, of course, a certain difficulty: ". . . the Viet Cong is
too strong to be simply beaten or suppressed." It follows, then,
that we must provide inducements to the Vietcong activists to
join our enterprise. This should not prove too difficult, he feels.
The Vietcong leadership consists basically of bureaucratic types
who are on the make. Cognitive dissonance theory suggests that
this "discontented leadership" has "the potential for making a
total break when the going gets too rough." We must therefore
provide them with "a political rationalization for changing
sides." The problem is ideological. We must induce a change in
the "image of reality" of the Vietcong cadres, replacing their
"naive ideology," which sees the GVN as "American puppets and
supporters of exploiters, the tax collectors, the merchants, the big
landlords, the police, and the evil men in the villages," by a more
realistic conception. We can do this by emphasizing hamlet
home rule and preventing the use of military forces to collect
rents, a suggestion which will be greeted with enthusiasm in
Saigon, no doubt. The opportunity to serve as functionaries for a
central government which pursues such policies will attract the

Vietcong cadres and thus solve our problem, that of excluding from the political process the organization that contains the effective political leaders.

Others have expressed a rather different evaluation of the human quality and motivation of these cadres. For example, Joseph Buttinger contrasts the inability of the Diem regime to mobilize support with the success of the NLF: "... that people willing to serve their country were to be found in Vietnam no one could doubt. The Vietminh had been able to enlist them by the tens of thousands and to extract from them superhuman efforts and sacrifices in the struggle for independence."[27] Military reports by the dozens relate the amazing heroism and dedication of the guerrillas. Throughout history, however, colonial administrators have had their difficulties in comprehending or coming to grips with this phenomenon.

In the course of his analysis of our dilemma in Vietnam, Pool explains some of the aspects of our culture that make it difficult for us to understand such matters clearly. We live in "a guilt culture in which there is a tradition of belief in equality." For such reasons, we find it hard to understand the true nature of Vietcong land redistribution, which is primarily "a patronage operation" in which "dissatisfied peasants band together in a gang to despoil their neighbors" and "then reward the deserving members of the cabal."

This terminology recalls Franz Borkenau's description of the "streak of moral indifference" in the history of Russian revolutionism, which permitted such atrocities as the willingness "to 'expropriate,' by means of robbery, the individual property of individual bourgeois."[28] Our side, in contrast, adheres to the "tradition of belief in equality" when we implement land reform. For example, the *New York Times,* December 26, 1967, reports a recent conference of experts studying the "Taiwan success in land reform," one of the real success stories of American intervention.

"The Government reimbursed the former landlords in part (30 per cent) with shares of four large public enterprises taken over from the Japanese. The remainder was paid in bonds. . . . Many speakers at the conference singled out the repayment as the shrewdest feature of the Taiwan program. It not only treated the landlords fairly, they said, but it also redirected the landlords' energies and capital towards industry," thus advancing the "wholesale restructuring of society" in the only healthy and humane direction.

In a side remark, Pool states that "in lay public debates now going on one often hears comments to the effect that Vietnamese communism, because it is anti-Chinese, would be like Yugoslav communism." It would, of course, be ridiculous to argue such a causal connection, and, in fact, I have never heard it proposed in "lay public debate" or anywhere else. Rather, what has been maintained by such laymen as Hans Morgenthau, General James Gavin, and others is that Vietnamese Communism is likely to be Titoist, in the sense that it will strive for independence from Chinese domination. Thus they reject the claim that by attacking Vietnamese Communism we are somehow "containing Chinese Communism"—a claim implied, for example, in the statement of the "Citizens Committee for Peace with Freedom in Vietnam," in which Ithiel Pool, Milton Sacks, and others, speaking for "the understanding, independent and responsible men and women who have consistently opposed rewarding international aggressors from Adolf Hitler to Mao Tse-tung," warn that if we "abandon Vietnam," then "Peking and Hanoi, flushed with success, [will] continue their expansionist policy through many other 'wars of liberation.' " By misstating the reference to Titoist tendencies, Pool avoids the difficulty of explaining how an anti-Chinese North Vietnam is serving as the agent of Hitlerian aggression from Peking; by referring to "lay public debate," he hopes, I presume, to disguise the failure of argument by a claim to expertise.

Returning again to the *Asian Survey* Vietnam symposium, the most significant contribution is surely Edward Mitchell's discussion of his RAND Corporation study on "the significance of land tenure in the Vietnamese insurgency." In a study of twenty-six provinces, Mitchell has discovered a significant correlation between "inequality of land tenure" and "extent of Government [read: American] control." In brief, "greater inequality implies greater control." "Provinces seem to be more secure when the percentage of owner-operated land is low (tenancy is high); inequality in the distribution of farms by size is great; large, formerly French-owned estates are present; and no land redistribution has taken place." To explain this phenomenon, Mitchell turns to history and behavioral psychology. As he notes, "in a number of historical cases it has been the better-to-do peasant who has revolted, while his poorer brothers actively supported or passively accepted the existing order." The "behavioral explanation" lies "in the relative docility of poorer peasants and the firm authority of landlords in the more 'feudal' areas . . . the landlord can exercise considerable influence over his tenant's behavior and readily discourage conduct inconsistent with his own interests."

In an interview with the *New York Times* (October 15, 1967), Mitchell adds an additional explanation for the fact that the most secure areas are those that remain "essentially feudal in social structure": when the feudal structure is eliminated, "there's a vacuum and that is ideal for the Vietcong because they've got an organization to fill the vacuum." This observation points to a difficulty that has always plagued the American effort. As Joseph Buttinger points out, the Diem regime too was unable to experiment with "freely constituted organizations" because these "would have been captured by the Vietminh." [29]

Mitchell's informative study supports an approach to counterinsurgency that has been expressed by Roger Hilsman, who explains that in his view, modernization "cannot help much in a counterguerrilla program," because it "inevitably uproots established social systems [and] produces political and economic dislocation and tension." He therefore feels that popularity of governments, reform, and modernization may be "important ingredients," but that their role in counterinsurgency "must be measured more in terms of their contributions to physical security."[30]

Before leaving this symposium on social science and Vietnam, we should take note of the scholarly detachment that permits one *not* to make certain comments or draw certain conclusions. For example, John Bennett discusses the important matter of "geographic and job mobility": "Under the dual impact of improved opportunities elsewhere and deteriorating security at home, people are willing to move to a hitherto unbelievable extent." No further comment on this "willingness," which provides such interesting new opportunities for the restructuring of Vietnamese society. John Donnell discusses the unusual success of pacification in Binh Dinh Province, particularly in the areas controlled by the Koreans, who "have tended to run their own show with their own methods and sometimes have not allowed the RD teams sent from Saigon all the operational leeway desired," and who have been "extremely impressive in eliminating NLF influence." Again, no comment is given on these methods, amply reported in the press,[31] or on the significance of the fact that Koreans are eliminating NLF influence from Vietnamese villages, and not allowing the Vietnamese government cadres the leeway desired.

Mitchell draws no policy conclusions from his study, but others have seen the point: recall the remarks of the moderate scholars on the dangers of social reform. Other scholars have carried the analysis much further. For example, Charles Wolf, senior economist of the RAND Corporation, discusses the matter in a recent book.[32] Wolf considers two "theoretical models" for analyzing insurgency problems. The first is the approach of the hearts-and-minds school of counterinsurgency, which emphasizes the importance of popular support. Wolf agrees that it is no doubt "a desirable goal" to win "popular allegiance to a government that is combating an insurgent movement," but this objective, he argues, is not appropriate "as a conceptual framework for counterinsurgency programs." His alternative approach has as its "unifying theme" the concept of "influencing *behavior,* rather than attitudes." Thus, "confiscation of chickens, razing of houses, or destruction of villages have a place in counterinsurgency efforts, but only if they are done for a strong reason: namely, to penalize those who have assisted the insurgents. . . . whatever harshness is meted out by government forces [must be] unambiguously recognizable as deliberately imposed because of behavior by the population that contributes to the insurgent movement." Furthermore, it must be noted that "policies that would increase rural income by raising food prices, or projects that would increase agricultural productivity through distribution of fertilizer or livestock, may be of negative value during an insurgency . . . since they may actually facilitate guerrilla operations by increasing the availability of inputs that the guerrillas need." More generally: "In setting up economic and social improvement programs, the crucial point is to connect such programs with the kind of population behavior the government wants to promote." The principle is to reward the villages that cooperate and to provide penalties for the behavior that the government is trying to discourage. "At a broad, conceptual level, the main concern of counterinsurgency efforts should be to influence the behavior of the population rather than their loyalties and attitudes"; "the primary consideration should be whether the proposed measure is likely to increase the cost and difficulties of insurgent operations and help to disrupt the insurgent organization, rather than whether it wins popular loyalty and support, or whether it contributes to a more productive, efficient, or equitable use of resources."

Other scholars have elaborated on the advantages of Wolf's "alternative approach," which concerns itself with control of behavior rather than the mystique of popular support. For example, Morton H. Halperin, of the Harvard Center for International Affairs, writes that in Vietnam, the United States "has been able to prevent any large-scale Vietcong victories, regardless of the loyalties of the people." Thus we have an empirical demonstration of a certain principle of behavioral science, as Halperin notes:

> The events in Vietnam also illustrate the fact that most people tend to be motivated, not by abstract appeals, but rather by their perception of the course of action that is most likely to lead to their own personal security and to the satisfaction of their economic, social, and psychological desires. Thus, for example, large-scale American bombing in South Vietnam may have antagonized a number of people; but at the same time it demonstrated to these people that the Vietcong could not guarantee their security as it had been able to do before the bombing and that the belief in an imminent victory for the Vietcong might turn out to be dangerously false.[33]

In short, along with "confiscation of chickens, razing of houses, or destruction of villages," we can also make effective use of 100 pounds of explosives per person, 12 tons per square mile, as in Vietnam, as a technique for controlling behavior, relying on the principle, now once again confirmed by experiment, that satisfaction of desires is a more important motivation in human behavior than abstract appeals to loyalty. Surely this is extremely sane advice. It would, for example, be absurd to try to control the behavior of a rat by winning its loyalty rather than by the proper scheduling of reinforcement.

An added advantage of this new, more scientific approach is that it will "modify the attitudes with which *counter*insurgency efforts are viewed in the United States"[34] (when we turn to the United States, of course, we are concerned with people whose attitudes must be taken into account, not merely their behavior). It will help us overcome one of the main defects in the American character, the "emotional reaction" that leads us to side with "crusaders for the common man" and against a "ruthless, exploitative tyrant" ("that there may be reality as well as appearance in this role-casting is not the point"). This sentimentality "frequently interferes with a realistic assessment of alternatives, and inclines us instead toward a carping righteousness in our relations with the beleaguered government we are ostensibly supporting"; it may be overcome by concentration on control of behavior rather than modification of attitudes or the winning of hearts and minds. Hence the new approach to counterinsurgency should not only be effective in extending the control of American-approved governments, but it may also have a beneficial effect on us. The possibilities are awe-inspiring. Perhaps in this way we can even escape the confines of our "guilt culture in which there is a tradition of belief in equality."

It is extremely important, Wolf would claim, that we develop a rational understanding of insurgency, for "insurgency is probably the most likely type of politico-military threat in the third world, and surely one of the most complex and challenging problems facing United States policies and programs." The primary objective of American foreign policy in the Third World must be "the *denial* of communist control," specifically, the support of countries that are defending their "independence from external and internal communist domination." The latter problem, defending

independence from internal Communist domination, is the crucial problem, particularly in Latin America. We must counter the
threat by a policy of promoting economic growth and modernization (making sure, however, to avoid the risks inherent in these
processes—cf. Mitchell), combined with "a responsible use of
force." No question is raised about the appropriateness of our use
of force in a country threatened by insurgency. The justification,
were the question raised, is inherent in the assumption that we
live "in a world in which loss of national independence is often
synonymous with communist control, and communism is im-
plicitly considered to be irreversible." Thus, by Orwellian logic,
we are actually defending national independence when we intervene with military force to protect a ruling elite from internal insurgency.[35]

Perhaps the most interesting aspect of scholarly work such as
this is the way in which behavioral-science rhetoric is used to
lend a vague aura of respectability. One might construct some
such chain of associations as this. Science, as everyone knows, is
responsible, moderate, unsentimental, and otherwise good. Behavioral science tells us that we can be concerned only with behavior and control of behavior. Therefore we *should* be
concerned only with behavior and control of behavior;[36] and it is
responsible, moderate, unsentimental, and otherwise good to
control behavior by appropriately applied reward and punish-
ment. Concern for loyalties and attitudes is emotional and unsci-
entific. As rational men, believers in the scientific ethic, we
should be concerned with manipulating behavior in a desirable
direction, and not be deluded by mystical notions of freedom, individual needs, or popular will.

Let me make it clear that I am not criticizing the behavioral
sciences because they lend themselves to such perversion. On
other grounds, the "behavioral persuasion" seems to me to lack
merit; it seriously mistakes the method of science and imposes

pointless methodological strictures on the study of man and society, but this is another matter entirely. It is, however, fair to inquire to what extent the popularity of this approach is based on its demonstrated achievements, and to what extent its appeal is based on the ease with which it can be refashioned as a new coercive ideology with a faintly scientific tone. (In passing, I think it is worth mention that the same questions can be raised outside of politics, specifically, in connection with education and therapy.)

The assumption that the colonial power is benevolent and has the interests of the natives at heart is as old as imperialism itself. Thus the liberal Herman Merivale, lecturing at Oxford in 1840, lauded the "British policy of colonial enlightenment" which "stands in contrast to that of our ancestors," who cared little "about the internal government of their colonies, and kept them in subjection in order to derive certain supposed commercial advantages from them," whereas we "give them commercial advantages, and tax ourselves for their benefit, in order to give them an interest in remaining under our supremacy, that we may have the pleasure of governing them."[37] And our own John Hay in 1898 outlined "a partnership in beneficence" which would bring freedom and civilization to Cuba, Hawaii, and the Philippines, just as the Pax Britannica had brought these benefits to India, Egypt, and South Africa.[38] But although the benevolence of imperialism is a familiar refrain, the idea that the issue of benevolence is irrelevant, an improper, sentimental consideration, is something of an innovation in imperialist rhetoric, a contribution of the sort one might perhaps expect from "the new mandarins" whose claim to power is based on knowledge and technique.

Going a step beyond, notice how perverse is the entire discussion of the "conceptual framework" for counterinsurgency. The idea that we must choose between the method of "winning hearts and minds" and the method of shaping behavior presumes that we have the right to choose at all. This is to grant us a right

that we would surely accord to no other world power. Yet the
overwhelming body of American scholarship accords us this
right. For example, William Henderson, formerly associate executive director and Far Eastern specialist for the Council on Foreign Relations, proposes that we must "prosecute a constructive,
manipulative diplomacy" in order to deal with "internal subversion, particularly in the form of Communist-instigated guerrilla
warfare or insurgency"—"internal aggression," as he calls it, in
accordance with contemporary usage.[39] Our "historic tasks," he
proclaims, are "nothing less than to assist purposefully and con-
structively in the processes of modern nation building in Southeast Asia, to deflect the course of a fundamental revolution into
channels compatible with the long range interests of the United
States." It is understood that true "nation building" is that path of
development compatible with our interests; hence there is no
difficulty in pursuing these historic tasks in concert. There are,
however, two real stumbling-blocks in the way of the required
manipulative diplomacy. The first is "a great psychological barrier." We must learn to abandon "old dogma" and pursue a "new
diplomacy" that is "frankly interventionist," recognizing "that it
goes counter to all the traditional conventions of diplomatic
usage." Some may ask whether "we have the moral right to interfere in the properly autonomous affairs of others," but Henderson feels that the Communist threat fully justifies such
interference and urges that we be ready to "use our 'special
forces' when the next bell rings," with no moral qualms or hesi-
tation. The second barrier is that "our knowledge is pitifully inadequate." He therefore calls on the academic community, which
will be only too willing to oblige, to supply "the body of expertise and the corps of specialists," the knowledge, the practitioners,
and the teachers, to enable us to conduct such a "resourceful
diplomacy" more effectively.

Turning to the liberal wing, we find that Roger Hilsman has a rather similar message in his study of the diplomacy of the Kennedy administration, *To Move a Nation*. He informs us that the most divisive issue among the "hardheaded and pragmatic liberals" of the Kennedy team was how the United States should deal with the problem of "modern guerrilla warfare, as the Communists practice it." The problem is that this "is *internal* war, an ambiguous aggression that avoids direct and open attack violating international frontiers" (italics his). Apparently, the hardheaded and pragmatic liberals were never divided on the issue of our right to violate international frontiers in reacting to such "internal war." As a prime example of the "kind of critical, searching analysis" that the new, liberal, revitalized State Department was trying to encourage, Hilsman cites a study directed to showing how the United States might have acted more effectively to overthrow the Mossadegh government in Iran. Allen Dulles was "fundamentally right," according to Hilsman, in judging that Mossadegh in Iran (like Arbenz in Guatemala) had come to power (to be sure, "through the usual processes of government") with "the intention of creating a Communist state"—a most amazing statement on the part of the State Department chief of intelligence; and Dulles was fundamentally right in urging support from the United States "to loyal anti-Communist elements" in Iran and Guatemala to meet the danger, even though "no invitation was extended by the *government* in power," obviously. Hilsman expresses the liberal view succinctly in the distinction he draws between the Iranian subversion and the blundering attempt at the Bay of Pigs: "It is one thing . . . to help the Shah's supporters in Iran in their struggle against Mossadegh and his Communist allies, but it is something else again to sponsor a thousand-man invasion against Castro's Cuba, where there was no effective internal opposition." The former effort was admirable; the latter, bound to fail, "is something else again" from the point of view of pragmatic liberalism.

In Vietnam liberal interventionism was not properly conducted, and the situation got out of hand. We learn more about
the character of this approach to international affairs by studying
a more successful instance. Thailand is a case in point, and a useful perspective on liberal American ideology is given by the careful and informative work of Frank C. Darling, a Kennedy liberal
who was a CIA analyst for Southeast Asia and is now chairman of
the political science department at DePauw University.[40]

The facts relevant to this discussion, as Darling outlines them,
are briefly as follows. At the end of World War II the former
British minister, Sir Josiah Crosby, warned that unless the power
of the Thai armed forces was reduced, "the establishment of a
constitutional government would be doomed and the return of a
military dictatorship would be inevitable." American policy in
the postwar period was to support and strengthen the armed
forces and the police, and Crosby's prediction was borne out.

There were incipient steps towards constitutional government
in the immediate postwar period. However, a series of military
coups established Phibun Songkhram, who had collaborated
with the Japanese during the war, as premier in 1948, aborting
these early efforts. The American reaction to the liberal governments had been ambiguous and "temporizing." In contrast, Phibun was immediately recognized by the United States. Why?
"Within this increasingly turbulent region Thailand was the only
nation that did not have a Communist insurrection within its
borders and it was the only country that remained relatively stable and calm. As the United States considered measures to deter
Communist aggression in Southeast Asia, a conservative and
anti-Communist regime in Thailand became increasingly attractive regardless of its internal policies or methods of achieving
power." Phibun got the point. In August 1949, "he stated that
foreign pressure had become 'alarming' and that internal Com-

munist activity had 'vigorously increased.' " In 1950, Truman approved a $10 million grant for military aid.

The new rulers made use of the substantial American military aid to convert the political system into "a more powerful and ruthless form of authoritarianism," and to develop an extensive system of corruption, nepotism, and profiteering that helped maintain the loyalty of their followers. At the same time, "American corporations moved in, purchasing large quantities of rubber and tin . . . shipments of raw materials now went directly to the United States instead of through Hong Kong and Singapore."[41] By 1958, "the United States purchased 90 percent of Thailand's rubber and most of its tin." American investment, however, remained low, because of the political instability as well as "the problems caused by more extensive public ownership and economic planning." To improve matters, the Sarit dictatorship (see below) introduced tax benefits and guarantees against nationalization and competition from government-owned commercial enterprises, and finally banned trade with China and abolished all monopolies, government or private, "in an attempt to attract private foreign capital."

American influence gave "material and moral support" to the Phibun dictatorship and "discouraged the political opposition." It strengthened the executive power and "encouraged the military leaders to take even stronger measures in suppressing local opposition, using the excuse that all anti-government activity was Communist-inspired." In 1954, Pridi Phanomyong, a liberal intellectual who had been the major participant in the overthrow of the absolute monarchy in 1932, had led the Free Thai underground during the war, and had been elected in 1946 when Thai democracy reached "an all-time high," appeared in Communist China; the United States was supporting Phibun, "who had been an ally of the Japanese, while Pridi, who had courageously assisted the OSS, was in Peking cooperating with the Chinese Communists." This was "ironic."

It is difficult to imagine what sort of development towards a constitutional, parliamentary system might have taken place had it not been for American-supported subversion. The liberals were extremely weak in any event, in particular because of the domination of the economy by Western and Chinese enterprises linked with the corrupt governmental bureaucracy. The Coup Group that had overthrown the government "was composed almost entirely of commoners, many of whom had come from the peasantry or low-ranking military and civil service families," and who now wanted their share in corruption and authoritarian control. The opposition "Democrats" were, for the most part, "members of the royal family or conservative landowners who wanted to preserve their role in the government and their personal wealth." Whatever opportunities might have existed for the development of some more equitable society disappeared once the American presence became dominant, however. Surely any Thai liberal reformer must have been aware of this by 1950, in the wake of the coups, the farcical rigged elections, the murder and torture of leaders of the Free Thai anti-Japanese underground, the takeover by the military of the political and much of the commercial system—particularly when he listened to the words of American Ambassador Stanton as he signed a new aid agreement: "The American people fully support this program of aid to Thailand because of their deep interest in the Thai people whose devotion to the ideals of freedom and liberty and whole-hearted support of the UN have won the admiration of the American people."

"A notable trend throughout this period was the growing intimacy between the Thai military leaders and the top-level military officials from the United States," who helped them obtain "large-scale foreign aid which in turn bolstered their political power." The head of the American military mission, Colonel Charles Sheldon, stated that Thailand was "threatened by armed aggression by people who do not believe in democracy, who do not believe in freedom or the dignity of the individual man as do the people of Thailand and my country." Adlai Stevenson, in 1953, warned the Thai leaders "that their country was the real target of the Vietminh," and expressed his hope that they "fully appreciate the threat." Meanwhile, United States assistance had built a powerful army and supplied the police with tanks, artillery, armored cars, an air force, naval patrol vessels, and a training school for paratroopers. The police achieved one of the highest ratios of policemen to citizens in the world—about 1 to 400. The police chief meanwhile relied on "his monopoly of the opium trade and his extensive commercial enterprises for the income he needed to support his personal political machine," while the army chief "received an enormous income from the national lottery."

It was later discovered that the chief of police had committed indescribable atrocities; "the extent of the torture and murder committed by the former police chief will probably never be known." What is known is what came to light after Sarit, the army chief, took power in a new coup in 1957. Sarit "stressed the need to maintain a stable government and intensify the suppression of local Communists to 'ensure continued American trust, confidence and aid.' " The Americans were naturally gratified, and the official reaction was very favorable. When Sarit died in 1963 it was discovered that his personal fortune reached perhaps $137 million. Both Darling and Roger Hilsman refer to him as a "benevolent" dictator, perhaps because he "realized that Communism could not be stopped solely by mass arrests, firing squads, or threats of brutal punishment, and launched a development project in the Northeast regions," along with various other mild reforms—without, however, ceasing the former practices, which he felt might "impress the Americans again with the need for more military and economic aid to prevent 'Communist' subversion." He also imposed rigid censorship, abolished trade organizations and labor unions and punished suspected "Communists" without mercy, and, as noted earlier, took various steps to attract foreign investment.

By 1960, "twelve percent of American foreign aid to Thailand since the beginning of the cold war had been devoted to economic and social advancement." The effect of the American aid was clear. "The vast material and diplomatic support provided to the military leaders by the United States helped to prevent the emergence of any competing groups who might check the trend toward absolute political rule and lead the country *back* to a more modern form of government" (italics mine). In fiscal 1963, the Kennedy administration tried to obtain from Congress $50 million in military aid for Thailand, perhaps to commemorate these achievements. The Kennedy administration brought "good intentions and well-founded policy proposals," but otherwise "made no significant modifications in the military-oriented policy in Thailand."

These excerpts give a fair picture of the American impact on Thailand, as it emerges from Darling's account. Naturally, he is not too happy about it. He is disturbed that American influence frustrated the moves towards constitutional democracy and contributed to an autocratic rule responsible for atrocities that sometimes "rivaled those of the Nazis and the Communists." He is also disturbed by our failure to achieve real control (in his terms, "security and stability") through these measures. Thus when Sarit took power in the 1957 coup, "the Americans had no assurance that he would not orient a new regime towards radical economic and social programs as Castro, for example, has done in Cuba. . . . At stake was an investment of about $300 million in military equipment and a gradually expanding economic base which could have been used against American interests in Southeast Asia had it fallen into unfriendly hands." Fortunately, these dire consequences did not ensue, and in place of radical economic and social programs there was merely a continuation of the same old terror and corruption. The danger was real, however.

What conclusions does Darling draw from this record? As he sees it,[42] there are four major alternatives for American foreign policy.

The first would be to "abolish its military program and withdraw American troops from the country." This, however, would be "irrational," because throughout the non-Communist world "respect for American patience and tolerance in dealing with nondemocratic governments would decline"; furthermore, "Thailand's security and economic progress would be jeopardized." To the pragmatic liberal, it is clear that confidence in our commitment to military dictatorships such as that in Thailand must be maintained, as in fact was implied by the moderate scholars' document discussed earlier; and it would surely be unfortunate to endanger the prospects for further development along the lines that were initiated in such a promising way under American influence, and that are now secured by some 40,000 American troops.

A second alternative would be neutralization of Thailand and other nations in Southeast Asia. This also is irrational. For one thing, "the withdrawal of the American military presence would not be matched by the removal of any Communist forces"— there being no nonindigenous Communist forces—and therefore we would gain nothing by this strategy. Furthermore, we could never be certain that there would not be "infiltration of Communist insurgents in the future." And finally, "the Thai leaders have decided to cooperate with the United States," for reasons that are hardly obscure.

A third alternative would be to use our power in Thailand to "push political and economic reforms." But this policy alternative would "do great damage to American strategy in Thailand and other non-Communist nations." And what is more, "extensive interference in the domestic affairs of other nations, no matter how well intentioned, is contrary to American traditions," as our postwar record in Thailand clearly demonstrates.[43]

Therefore, we must turn to the fourth alternative, and maintain our present policy. "This alternative is probably the most rational and realistic. The military policy can be enhanced if it is realized that only American military power is capable of preventing large-scale overt aggression in Southeast Asia, and the proper role for the Thai armed forces is to be prepared to cope with limited guerrilla warfare."

This exposition of United States policy in Thailand and the directions it should take conforms rather well to the general lines of pragmatic liberalism as drawn by Hilsman, among others. It also indicates clearly the hope that we offer today to the countries on the fringes of Asia. Vietnam may be an aberration. Our impact on Thailand, however, can hardly be attributed to the politics of inadvertence.

An interesting sidelight is Darling's explanation in *Thailand and the United States* of how, in an earlier period, "the Western concept of the rule of law" was disseminated through American influence. "Evidence that some officials were obtaining an understanding of the rule of law was revealed" by the statement of a Thai minister who pointed out that "it is essential to the prosperity of a nation that it should have fixed laws, and that nobles should be restrained from oppressing the people, otherwise the latter were like chickens, who instead of being kept for their eggs, were killed off." In its international behavior as well, the Thai government came to understand the necessity for the rule of law: "A growing respect for law was also revealed in the adherence of the Thai government to the unequal restrictions contained in the treaties with the Western nations in spite of the heavy burden they imposed on the finances of the kingdom." This is all said without irony. In fact, the examples clarify nicely what the "rule of law" means to weak nations, and to the exploited in any society.

Darling, Hilsman, and many others whom I have been discussing represent the moderate liberal wing of scholarship on international affairs. It may be useful to sample some of the other views that appear in American scholarship. Consider, for example, the proposals of Thomas R. Adam, professor of political science at New York University.[44]

Adam begins by outlining an "ideal solution" to American problems in the Pacific, towards which we should bend our efforts. The ideal solution would have the United States recognized as "the responsible military protagonist of all Western interests in the area" with a predominant voice in a unified Western policy. United States sovereignty over some territorial base in the area would give us "ideal conditions for extending power over adjoining regions." Such a base would permit the formation of a regional organization, under our dominance, that would make possible "direct intervention in Korea, Vietnam, Laos and Cambodia" without the onus of unilateral intervention ("in the face of brazen communist aggression, it is not the fact of intervention as such that constitutes the issue but rather its unilateral character").

We must understand that for the preservation of Western interests, there is no reasonable alternative to the construction of such a base of power in territories over which we possess direct sovereignty. We cannot maintain the "historic connection" between Asia and the West unless we participate in Asian affairs "through the exercise of power and influence." We must accept "the fact that we are engaged in a serious struggle for cultural

survival that involves that continuous presence of Western-
oriented communities" in Asia. It is an illusion to believe that we
can retreat from Asia and leave it to its own devices, for our own
Western culture must be understood as "a minority movement
of recent date in the evolution of civilization," and it cannot be
taken for granted that Asia will remain "incapable of intervening
in our affairs." Thus to defend ourselves, we must intervene with
force in the affairs of Asia. If we fail to establish "our industrial
enterprise system" universally, we will have to "defend our priv-
ileges and gains by means of the continuing, brutalizing, and
costly exercise of superior force in every corner of the globe."

Why are we justified in forceful intervention in the affairs of
Asia? "One obvious justification for United States intervention
in Asian affairs lies in our leadership of the world struggle against
communism. Communist political and economic infiltration
among a majority of the world's peoples appears to American
political leadership to be fatal to our safety and progress; this attitude is supported almost unanimously by public opinion." Pursuing this logic a few steps further, we will soon have the same
"obvious justification" for taking out China with nuclear
weapons—and perhaps France as well, for good measure.

Further justification is that the defense of our western
seaboard "requires that the North Pacific be controlled as a virtual American lake," a fact which "provides one basis for United
States intervention in power struggles throughout the region," to
preserve the security of this *mare nostrum*. Our "victory over
Japan left a power vacuum in Southeast Asia and the Far East that
was tempting to communist aggression; therefore, we had to step
in and use our military power." "Island possessions, such as
Guam, those of the strategic trust territories, and probably Oki-
nawa, remain indispensable, if not to the narrow defense of our
shores, certainly to the military posture essential to our total security and world aims." [45] Apart from the magnificent scope of

this vision, rarely equaled by our forerunners, the terminology is not unfamiliar.

There are, to be sure, certain restraints that we must observe as we design our policy of establishing an "operational base" for exercise of power in the Far East; specifically, "policy must rest on political and social objectives that are acceptable to, or capable of being imposed upon, all participating elements." Obviously, it would not be pragmatic to insist upon policies that are not capable of being imposed upon the participating elements in our new dominions.

These proposals are buttressed with a brief sketch of the consequences of Western dominion in the past, for example, the "Indian success story," in which "enterprise capital proved a useful incentive to fruitful social change in the subcontinent of India and its environs," a development flawed only by the passivity shown by "traditional Asian social systems" as they imitated "the industrial ideology of their colonial tutor." An important lesson to us is the success of the "neutral Pax Britannica" in imposing order, so that "commerce could flourish and its fruits compensate for vanished liberties."

Adam spares us the observation that the ungrateful natives sometimes fail to appreciate these centuries of solicitude. Thus to a left-wing member of the Congress party in India: "The story is that the British, in the process of their domination over India, kept no limits to brutality and savagery which man is capable of practicing. Hitler's depredations, his Dachaus and Belsens . . . pale into insignificance before this imperialist savagery. . . ." [46] Such a reaction to centuries of selfless and tender care might cause some surprise, until we realize that it is probably only an expression of the enormous guilt felt by the beneficiary of these attentions.

A generation ago, there were other political leaders who feared the effect of Communist gains on their safety and progress, and who, with the almost unanimous support of public opinion, set out to improve the world through forceful intervention—filling power vacuums, establishing territorial bases essential to their total security and world aims, imposing political and social objectives on participating elements. Professor Adam has little to tell us that is new.

II

The examples of counterrevolutionary subordination that I have so far cited have for the most part been drawn from political science and the study of international, particularly Asian, affairs—rather dismal branches of American scholarship, by and large, and so closely identified with American imperial goals that one is hardly astonished to discover the widespread abandonment of civilized norms. In opening this discussion, however, I referred to a far more general issue. If it is plausible that ideology will in general serve as a mask for self-interest, then it is a natural presumption that intellectuals, in interpreting history or formulating policy, will tend to adopt an elitist position, condemning popular movements and mass participation in decision making, and emphasizing rather the necessity for supervision by those who possess the knowledge and understanding that is required (so they claim) to manage society and control social change. This is hardly a novel thought. One major element in the anarchist critique of Marxism a century ago was the prediction that, as Bakunin formulated it:

> According to the theory of Mr. Marx, the people not only must not destroy [the state] but must strengthen it and place it at the complete disposal of their benefactors, guardians, and teachers— the leaders of the Communist party, namely Mr. Marx and his friends, who will proceed to liberate [mankind] in their own way.

They will concentrate the reins of government in a strong hand, because the ignorant people require an exceedingly firm guardianship; they will establish a single state bank, concentrating in its hands all commercial, industrial, agricultural and even scientific production, and then divide the masses into two armies—industrial and agricultural—under the direct command of the state engineers, who will constitute a new privileged scientific-political estate.[47]

One cannot fail to be struck by the parallel between this prediction and that of Daniel Bell, cited earlier—the prediction that in the new postindustrial society, "not only the best talents, but eventually the entire complex of social prestige and social status, will be rooted in the intellectual and scientific communities."[48] Pursuing the parallel for a moment, it might be asked whether the left-wing critique of Leninist elitism can be applied, under very different conditions, to the liberal ideology of the intellectual elite that aspires to a dominant role in managing the welfare state.

Rosa Luxemburg, in 1918, argued that Bolshevik elitism would lead to a state of society in which the bureaucracy alone would remain an active element in social life—though now it would be the "red bureaucracy" of that State Socialism that Bakunin had long before described as "the most vile and terrible lie that our century has created."[49] A true social revolution requires a "spiritual transformation in the masses degraded by centuries of bourgeois class rule";[50] "it is only by extirpating the habits of obedience and servility to the last root that the working class can acquire the understanding of a new form of discipline, self-discipline arising from free consent."[51] Writing in 1904, she predicted that Lenin's organizational concepts would "enslave a young labor movement to an intellectual elite hungry for power . . . and turn it into an automaton manipulated by a Central

Committee." [52] In the Bolshevik elitist doctrine of 1918 she saw a disparagement of the creative, spontaneous, self-correcting force of mass action, which alone, she argued, could solve the thousand problems of social reconstruction and produce the spiritual transformation that is the essence of a true social revolution. As Bolshevik practice hardened into dogma, the fear of popular initiative and spontaneous mass action, not under the direction and control of the properly designated vanguard, became a dominant element of so-called "Communist" ideology.

Antagonism to mass movements and to social change that escapes the control of privileged elites is also a prominent feature of contemporary liberal ideology. [53] Expressed as foreign policy, it takes the form described earlier. To conclude this discussion of counterrevolutionary subordination, I would like to investigate how, in one rather crucial case, this particular bias in American liberal ideology can be detected even in the interpretation of events of the past in which American involvement was rather slight, and in historical work of very high caliber.

In 1966, the American Historical Association gave its biennial award for the most outstanding work on European history to Gabriel Jackson, for his study of Spain in the 1930s. [54] There is no question that of the dozens of books on this period, Jackson's is among the best, and I do not doubt that the award was well deserved. The Spanish Civil War is one of the crucial events of modern history, and one of the most extensively studied as well. In it, we find the interplay of forces and ideas that have dominated European history since the industrial revolution. What is more, the relationship of Spain to the great powers was in many respects like that of the countries of what is now called the Third World. In some ways, then, the events of the Spanish Civil War give a foretaste of what the future may hold, as Third World revolutions uproot traditional societies, threaten imperial dominance, exacerbate great-power rivalries, and bring the world perilously close to a war which, if not averted, will surely be the final catastrophe of modern history. My reason for wanting to investigate an outstanding liberal analysis of the Spanish Civil War is therefore twofold: first, because of the intrinsic interest of these events; and second, because of the insight that this analysis may provide with respect to the underlying elitist bias which I believe to be at the root of the phenomenon of counterrevolutionary subordination.

In his study of the Spanish Republic, Jackson makes no attempt to hide his own commitment in favor of liberal democracy, as represented by such figures as Azaña, Casares Quiroga, Martínez Barrio,[55] and the other "responsible national leaders." In taking this position, he speaks for much of liberal scholarship; it is fair to say that figures similar to those just mentioned would be supported by American liberals, were this possible, in Latin America, Asia, or Africa. Furthermore, Jackson makes little attempt to disguise his antipathy towards the forces of popular revolution in Spain, or their goals.

It is no criticism of Jackson's study that his point of view and sympathies are expressed with such clarity. On the contrary, the value of this work as an interpretation of historical events is enhanced by the fact that the author's commitments are made so clear and explicit. But I think it can be shown that Jackson's account of the popular revolution that took place in Spain is misleading and in part quite unfair, and that the failure of objectivity it reveals is highly significant in that it is characteristic of the attitude taken by liberal (and Communist) intellectuals towards revolutionary movements that are largely spontaneous and only loosely organized, while rooted in deeply felt needs and ideals of dispossessed masses. It is a convention of scholarship that the use of such terms as those of the preceding phrase demonstrates naiveté and muddle-headed sentimentality. The convention, however, is supported by ideological conviction rather than his-

tory or investigation of the phenomena of social life. This conviction is, I think, belied by such events as the revolution that
swept over much of Spain in the summer of 1936.

The circumstances of Spain in the 1930s are not duplicated
elsewhere in the underdeveloped world today, to be sure. Nevertheless, the limited information that we have about popular
movements in Asia, specifically, suggests certain similar features
that deserve much more serious and sympathetic study than they
have so far received.[56] Inadequate information makes it haz-
ardous to try to develop any such parallel, but I think it is quite
possible to note long-standing tendencies in the response of liberal as well as Communist intellectuals to such mass movements.

As I have already remarked, the Spanish Civil War is not only
one of the critical events of modern history but one of the most
intensively studied as well. Yet there are surprising gaps. During
the months following the Franco insurrection in July 1936, a social revolution of unprecedented scope took place throughout
much of Spain. It had no "revolutionary vanguard" and appears
to have been largely spontaneous, involving masses of urban and
rural laborers in a radical transformation of social and economic
conditions that persisted, with remarkable success, until it was
crushed by force. This predominantly anarchist revolution and
the massive social transformation to which it gave rise are treated,
in recent historical studies, as a kind of aberration, a nuisance that
stood in the way of successful prosecution of the war to save the
bourgeois regime from the Franco rebellion. Many historians
would probably agree with Eric Hobsbawm[57] that the *failure* of
social revolution in Spain "was due to the anarchists," that anarchism was "a disaster," a kind of "moral gymnastics" with no
"concrete results," at best "a profoundly moving spectacle for the
student of popular religion." The most extensive historical study
of the anarchist revolution[58] is relatively inaccessible, and neither
its author, now living in southern France, nor the many refugees

who will never write memoirs but who might provide invaluable personal testimony have been consulted, apparently, by writers of the major historical works.[59] The one published collection of documents dealing with collectivization[60] has been published only by an anarchist press and hence is barely accessible to the general reader, and has also rarely been consulted—it does not, for example, appear in Jackson's bibliography, though Jackson's account is intended to be a social and political, not merely a military, history. In fact, this astonishing social upheaval seems to have largely passed from memory. The drama and pathos of the Spanish Civil War have by no means faded; witness the impact a few years ago of the film *To Die in Madrid*. Yet in this film (as Daniel Guérin points out) one finds no reference to the popular revolution that had transformed much of Spanish society.

I will be concerned here with the events of 1936–1937,[61] and with one particular aspect of the complex struggle involving Franco Nationalists, Republicans (including the Communist party), anarchists, and socialist workers' groups. The Franco insurrection in July 1936 came against a background of several months of strikes, expropriations, and battles between peasants and Civil Guards. The left-wing Socialist leader Largo Caballero had demanded in June that the workers be armed, but was refused by Azaña. When the coup came, the Republican government was paralyzed. Workers armed themselves in Madrid and Barcelona, robbing government armories and even ships in the harbor, and put down the insurrection while the government vacillated, torn between the twin dangers of submitting to Franco and arming the working classes. In large areas of Spain effective authority passed into the hands of the anarchist and socialist workers who had played a substantial, generally dominant role in putting down the insurrection.

The next few months have frequently been described as a period of "dual power." In Barcelona industry and commerce were

largely collectivized, and a wave of collectivization spread
through rural areas, as well as towns and villages, in Aragon,
Castile, and the Levant, and to a lesser but still significant extent
in many parts of Catalonia, Asturias, Estremadura, and Andalusia.
Military power was exercised by defense committees; social and
economic organization took many forms, following in main outlines the program of the Saragossa Congress of the anarchist
CNT in May 1936. The revolution was "apolitical," in the sense
that its organs of power and administration remained separate
from the central Republican government and, even after several
anarchist leaders entered the government in the autumn of 1936,
continued to function fairly independently until the revolution
was finally crushed between the fascist and Communist-led Republican forces. The success of collectivization of industry and
commerce in Barcelona impressed even highly unsympathetic
observers such as Borkenau. The scale of rural collectivization is
indicated by these data from anarchist sources: in Aragon, 450
collectives with half a million members; in the Levant, 900 collectives accounting for about half the agricultural production and
70 percent of marketing in this, the richest agricultural region of
Spain; in Castile, 300 collectives with about 100,000 members.[62]
In Catalonia, the bourgeois government headed by Companys
retained nominal authority, but real power was in the hands of
the anarchist-dominated committees.

The period of July through September may be characterized
as one of spontaneous, widespread, but unconsummated social
revolution.[63] A number of anarchist leaders joined the government; the reason, as stated by Federica Montseny on January 3,
1937, was this: ". . . the anarchists have entered the government
to prevent the Revolution from deviating and in order to carry it
further beyond the war, and also to oppose any dictatorial tendency, from wherever it might come."[64] The central government
fell increasingly under Communist control—in Catalonia, under

the control of the Communist-dominated PSUC—largely as a result of the valuable Russian military assistance. Communist success was greatest in the rich farming areas of the Levant (the government moved to Valencia, capital of one of the provinces), where prosperous farm owners flocked to the Peasant Federation that the party had organized to protect the wealthy farmers; this federation "served as a powerful instrument in checking the rural collectivization promoted by the agricultural workers of the province."[65] Elsewhere as well, counterrevolutionary successes reflected increasing Communist dominance of the Republic.

The first phase of the counterrevolution was the legalization and regulation of those accomplishments of the revolution that appeared irreversible. A decree of October 7 by the Communist Minister of Agriculture, Vicente Uribe, legalized certain expro-priations—namely, of lands belonging to participants in the Franco revolt. Of course, these expropriations had already taken place, a fact that did not prevent the Communist press from de-scribing the decree as "the most profoundly revolutionary mea-sure that has been taken since the military uprising."[66] In fact, by exempting the estates of landowners who had not directly partic-ipated in the Franco rebellion, the decree represented a step back-ward, from the standpoint of the revolutionaries, and it was criticized not only by the CNT but also by the Socialist Federa-tion of Land Workers, affiliated with the UGT. The demand for a much broader decree was unacceptable to the Communist-led ministry, since the Communist party was "seeking support among the propertied classes in the anti-Franco coup" and hence "could not afford to repel the small and medium proprietors who had been hostile to the working class movement before the civil war."[67] These "small proprietors," in fact, seem to have included owners of substantial estates. The decree compelled tenants to continue paying rent unless the landowners had supported Franco, and by guaranteeing former landholdings, it prevented distribution of land to the village poor. Ricardo Zabalza, general secretary of the Federation of Land Workers, described the resulting situation as one of "galling injustice"; "the sycophants of the former political bosses still enjoy a privileged position at the expense of those persons who were unable to rent even the smallest parcel of land, because they were revolutionaries."[68]

To complete the stage of legalization and restriction of what had already been achieved, a decree of October 24, 1936, promulgated by a CNT member who had become Councilor for Economy in the Catalonian Generalitat, gave legal sanction to the collectivization of industry in Catalonia. In this case too, the step was regressive, from the revolutionary point of view. Collectivization was limited to enterprises employing more than a hundred workers, and a variety of conditions were established that removed control from the workers' committees to the state bureaucracy.[69]

The second stage of the counterrevolution, from October 1936 through May 1937, involved the destruction of the local committees, the replacement of the militia by a conventional army, and the re-establishment of the prerevolutionary social and economic system, wherever this was possible. Finally, in May 1937, came a direct attack on the working class in Barcelona (the May Days).[70] Following the success of this attack, the process of liquidation of the revolution was completed. The collectivization decree of October 24 was rescinded and industries were "freed" from workers' control. Communist-led armies swept through Aragon, destroying many collectives and dismantling their organizations and, generally, bringing the area under the control of the central government. Throughout the Republican-held territories, the government, now under Communist domination, acted in accordance with the plan announced in *Pravda* on December 17, 1936: "So far as Catalonia is concerned, the cleaning up of Trotzkyist and Anarcho-Syndicalist elements there has already begun, and it will be carried out there with the same energy as in the U.S.S.R."[71]—and, we may add, in much the same manner.

In brief, the period from the summer of 1936 to 1937 was one of revolution and counterrevolution: the revolution was largely spontaneous with mass participation of anarchist and socialist industrial and agricultural workers; the counterrevolution was under Communist direction, the Communist party increasingly coming to represent the right wing of the Republic. During this period and after the success of the counterrevolution, the Republic was waging a war against the Franco insurrection; this has been described in great detail in numerous publications, and I will say little about it here. The Communist-led counterrevolutionary struggle must, of course, be understood against the background of the ongoing antifascist war and the more general attempt of the Soviet Union to construct a broad antifascist alliance with the Western democracies. One reason for the vigorous counterrevolutionary policy of the Communists was their belief that England would never tolerate a revolutionary triumph in Spain, where England had substantial commercial interests, as did France and to a lesser extent the United States.[72] I will return to this matter below. However, I think it is important to bear in mind that there were undoubtedly other factors as well. Rudolf Rocker's comments are, I believe, quite to the point:

> . . . the Spanish people have been engaged in a desperate struggle against a pitiless foe and have been exposed besides to the secret intrigues of the great imperialist powers of Europe. Despite this the Spanish revolutionaries have not grasped at the disastrous expedient of dictatorship, but have respected all honest convictions. Everyone who visited Barcelona after the July battles, whether friend or foe of the C.N.T., was surprised at the freedom

of public life and the absence of any arrangements for suppressing the free expression of opinion.

For two decades the supporters of Bolshevism have been hammering it into the masses that dictatorship is a vital necessity for the defense of the so-called proletarian interests against the assaults of the counter-revolution and for paving the way for Socialism. They have not advanced the cause of Socialism by this propaganda, but have merely smoothed the way for Fascism in Italy, Germany and Austria by causing millions of people to forget that dictatorship, the most extreme form of tyranny, can never lead to social liberation. In Russia, the so-called dictatorship of the proletariat has not led to Socialism, but to the domination of a new bureaucracy over the proletariat and the whole people. . . .

What the Russian autocrats and their supporters fear most is that the success of libertarian Socialism in Spain might prove to their blind followers that the much vaunted "necessity of a dictatorship" is nothing but one vast fraud which in Russia has led to the despotism of Stalin and is to serve today in Spain to help the counter-revolution to a victory over the revolution of the workers and peasants.[73]

After decades of anti-Communist indoctrination, it is difficult to achieve a perspective that makes possible a serious evaluation of the extent to which Bolshevism and Western liberalism have been united in their opposition to popular revolution. However, I do not think that one can comprehend the events in Spain without attaining this perspective.

With this brief sketch—partisan, but I think accurate—for background, I would like to turn to Jackson's account of this aspect of the Spanish Civil War (see note 54).

Jackson presumes (p. 259) that Soviet support for the Republican cause in Spain was guided by two factors: first, concern for Soviet security; second, the hope that a Republican victory would advance "the cause of worldwide 'people's revolution' with which Soviet leaders hoped to identify themselves." They did not press their revolutionary aims, he feels, because "for the moment it was essential not to frighten the middle classes or the Western governments."

As to the concern for Soviet security, Jackson is no doubt correct. It is clear that Soviet support of the Republic was one aspect of the attempt to make common cause with the Western democracies against the fascist threat. However, Jackson's conception of the Soviet Union as a revolutionary power—hopeful that a Republican victory would advance "the interrupted movement toward world revolution" and seeking to identify itself with "the cause of the world-wide 'people's revolution' "—seems to me entirely mistaken. Jackson presents no evidence to support this interpretation of Soviet policy, nor do I know of any. It is interesting to see how differently the events were interpreted at the time of the Spanish Civil War, not only by anarchists like Rocker but also by such commentators as Gerald Brenan and Franz Borkenau, who were intimately acquainted with the situation in Spain. Brenan observes that the counter-revolutionary policy of the Communists (which he thinks was "extremely sensible") was

> the policy most suited to the Communists themselves. Russia is a totalitarian regime ruled by a bureaucracy: the frame of mind of its leaders, who have come through the most terrible upheaval in history, is cynical and opportunist: the whole fabric of the state is dogmatic and authoritarian. To expect such men to lead a social revolution in a country like Spain, where the wildest idealism is combined with great independence of character, was out of the question. The Russians could, it is true, command plenty of idealism among their foreign admirers, but they could only harness it to the creation of a cast-iron bureaucratic state, where everyone thinks alike and obeys the orders of the chief above him.[74]

He sees nothing in Russian conduct in Spain to indicate any interest in a "people's revolution." Rather, the Communist policy was to oppose "even such rural and industrial collectives as had risen spontaneously and flood the country with police who, like the Russian Ogpu, acted on the orders of their party rather than those of the Ministry of the Interior." The Communists were concerned to suppress altogether the impulses towards "spontaneity of speech or action," since "their whole nature and history made them distrust the local and spontaneous and put their faith in order, discipline and bureaucratic uniformity"—hence placed them in opposition to the revolutionary forces in Spain. As Brenan also notes, the Russians withdrew their support once it became clear that the British would not be swayed from the policy of appeasement, a fact which gives additional confirmation to the thesis that only considerations of Russian foreign policy led the Soviet Union to support the Republic.

Borkenau's analysis is similar. He approves of the Communist policy, because of its "efficiency," but he points out that the Communists "put an end to revolutionary social activity, and enforced their view that this ought not to be a revolution but simply the defence of a legal government. . . . communist policy in Spain was mainly dictated not by the necessities of the Spanish fight but by the interests of the intervening foreign power, Russia," a country "with a revolutionary past, not a revolutionary present." The Communists acted "not with the aim of transforming chaotic enthusiasm into disciplined enthusiasm [which Borkenau feels to have been necessary], but with the aim of substituting disciplined military and administrative action for the action of the masses and getting rid of the latter entirely." This policy, he points out, went "directly against the interests and claims of the masses" and thus weakened popular support. The now apathetic masses would not commit themselves to the defense of a Communist-run dictatorship, which restored former authority and even "showed a definite preference for the police forces of the old regime, so hated by the masses." It seems to me that the record strongly supports this interpretation of Communist policy and its effects, though Borkenau's assumption that Communist "efficiency" was necessary to win the anti-Franco struggle is much more dubious—a question to which I return below.[75]

It is relevant to observe, at this point, that a number of the Spanish Communist leaders were reluctantly forced to similar conclusions. Bolloten cites several examples,[76] specifically, the military commander "El Campesino" and Jesús Hernández, a minister in the Caballero government. The former, after his escape from the Soviet Union in 1949, stated that he had taken for granted the "revolutionary solidarity" of the Soviet Union during the Civil War—a most remarkable degree of innocence—and realized only later "that the Kremlin does not serve the interests of the peoples of the world, but makes them serve its own interests; that, with a treachery and hypocrisy without parallel, it makes use of the international working class as a mere pawn in its political intrigues." Hernández, in a speech given shortly after the Civil War, admits that the Spanish Communist leaders "acted more like Soviet subjects than sons of the Spanish people." "It may seem absurd, incredible," he adds, "but our education under Soviet tutelage had deformed us to such an extent that we were completely denationalized; our national soul was torn out of us and replaced by a rabidly chauvinistic internationalism, which began and ended with the towers of the Kremlin."

Shortly after the Third World Congress of the Communist International in 1921, the Dutch "ultra-leftist" Hermann Gorter wrote that the congress "has decided the fate of the world revolution for the present. The trend of opinion that seriously desired world revolution . . . has been expelled from the Russian International. The Communist Parties in western Europe and throughout the world that retain their membership of the Russian International will become nothing more than a means to preserve the Russian Revolution and the Soviet Republic."[77] This forecast has proved quite accurate. Jackson's conception that the Soviet Union was a revolutionary power in the late 1930s, or even that the Soviet leaders truly regarded themselves as identified with world revolution, is without factual support. It is a misinterpretation that runs parallel to the American Cold War mythology that has invented an "international Communist conspiracy" directed from Moscow (now Peking) to justify its own interventionist policies.

Turning to events in revolutionary Spain, Jackson describes the first stages of collectivization as follows: the unions in Madrid, "as in Barcelona and Valencia, abused their sudden authority to place the sign *incautado* [placed under workers' control] on all manner of buildings and vehicles" (p. 279). Why was this an *abuse* of authority? This Jackson does not explain. The choice of words indicates a reluctance on Jackson's part to recognize the reality of the revolutionary situation, despite his account of the breakdown of Republican authority. The statement that the workers "abused their sudden authority" by carrying out collectivization rests on a moral judgment that recalls that of Ithiel Pool, when he characterizes land reform in Vietnam as a matter of "despoiling one's neighbors," or of Franz Borkenau, when he speaks of expropriation in the Soviet Union as "robbery," demonstrating "a streak of moral indifference."

Within a few months, Jackson informs us, "the revolutionary tide began to ebb in Catalonia" after "accumulating food and supply problems, and the experience of administering villages, frontier posts, and public utilities, had rapidly shown the anarchists the unsuspected complexity of modern society" (pp. 313–14). In Barcelona, "the naïve optimism of the revolutionary conquests of the previous August had given way to feelings of resentment and of somehow having been cheated," as the cost of living doubled, bread was in short supply, and police brutality reached the levels of the monarchy. "The POUM and the anarchist press simultaneously extolled the collectivizations and explained the failures of production as due to Valencia policies of boycotting the Catalan economy and favoring the *bourgeoisie*. They explained the loss of Málaga as due in large measure to the low morale and the disorientation of the Andalusian proletariat, which saw the Valencia government evolving steadily toward the right" (p. 368). Jackson evidently believes that this left-wing interpretation of events was nonsensical, and that in fact it was anarchist incompetence or treachery that was responsible for the difficulties: "In Catalonia, the CNT factory committees dragged their heels on war production, claiming that the government deprived them of raw materials and was favoring the *bourgeoisie*" (p. 365).

In fact, "the revolutionary tide began to ebb in Catalonia" under a middle-class attack led by the Communist party, not because of a recognition of the "complexity of modern society." And it was, moreover, quite true that the Communist-dominated central government attempted, with much success, to hamper collectivized industry and agriculture and to disrupt the collectivization of commerce. I have already referred to the early stages of counterrevolution. Further investigation of the sources to which Jackson refers and others shows that the anarchist charges were not baseless, as Jackson implies. Bolloten cites a good deal of evidence in support of his conclusion that

> In the countryside the Communists undertook a spirited defence of the small and medium proprietor and tenant farmer against the collectivizing drive of the rural wage-workers, against the policy of the labour unions prohibiting the farmer from holding more land than he could cultivate with his own hands, and against the

practices of revolutionary committees, which requisitioned harvests, interfered with private trade, and collected rents from tenant farmers.[78]

The policy of the government was clearly enunciated by the Communist Minister of Agriculture: "We say that the property of the small farmer is sacred and that those who attack or attempt to attack this property must be regarded as enemies of the regime."[79] Gerald Brenan, no sympathizer with collectivization, explains the failure of collectivization as follows (p. 321):

> The Central Government, and especially the Communist and Socialist members of it, desired to bring [the collectives] under the direct control of the State: they therefore failed to provide them with the credit required for buying raw materials: as soon as the supply of raw cotton was exhausted the mills stopped working. . . . even [the munitions industry in Catalonia] were harassed by the new bureaucratic organs of the Ministry of Supply.[80]

He quotes the bourgeois President of Catalonia, Companys, as saying that "workers in the arms factories in Barcelona had been working 56 hours and more each week and that no cases of sabotage or indiscipline had taken place," until the workers were demoralized by the bureaucratization—later, militarization—imposed by the central government and the Communist party.[81] His own conclusion is that "the Valencia Government was now using the P.S.U.C. against the C.N.T.—but not . . . because the Catalan workers were giving trouble, but because the Communists wished to weaken them before destroying them."

The cited correspondence from Companys to Prieto, according to Vernon Richards (p. 47), presents evidence showing the success of Catalonian war industry under collectivization and demonstrating how "much more could have been achieved had the means for expanding the industry not been denied them by the Central Government." Richards also cites testimony by a spokesman for the subsecretariat of munitions and armament of the Valencia government admitting that "the war industry of Catalonia had produced ten times more than the rest of Spanish industry put together and [agreeing] . . . that this output could have been quadrupled as from beginning of September⋆ if Catalonia had had access to the necessary means for purchasing raw materials that were unobtainable in Spanish territory." It is important to recall that the central government had enormous gold reserves (soon to be transmitted to the Soviet Union), so that raw materials for Catalan industry could probably have been purchased, despite the hostility of the Western democracies to the Republic during the revolutionary period (see below). Furthermore, raw materials had repeatedly been requested. On September 24, 1936, Juan Fabregas, the CNT delegate to the Economic Council of Catalonia who was in part responsible for the collectivization decree cited earlier, reported that the financial difficulties of Catalonia were created by the refusal of the central government to "give any assistance in economic and financial questions, presumably because it has little sympathy with the work of a practical order which is being carried out in Catalonia"[82]—that is, collectivization. He "went on to recount that a Commission which went to Madrid to ask for credits to purchase war materials and raw materials, offering 1,000 million pesetas in securities lodged in the Bank of Spain, met with a blank refusal. It was sufficient that the new war industry in Catalonia was controlled by the workers of the C.N.T. for the Madrid Government to refuse any unconditional aid. Only in exchange for government control would they give financial assistance."[83]

Broué and Témime take a rather similar position. Comment-

⋆ The quoted testimony is from September 1, 1937; presumably, the reference is to September 1936.

ing on the charge of "incompetence" leveled against the collectivized industries, they point out that "one must not neglect the
terrible burden of the war." Despite this burden, they observe,
"new techniques of management and elimination of dividends
had permitted a lowering of prices" and "mechanisation and rationalization, introduced in numerous enterprises . . . had con-
siderably augmented production. The workers accepted the
enormous sacrifices with enthusiasm because, in most cases, they
had the conviction that the factory belonged to them and that at
last they were working for themselves and their class brothers. A
truly new spirit had come over the economy of Spain with the
concentration of scattered enterprises, the simplification of commercial patterns, a significant structure of social projects for aged
workers, children, disabled, sick and the personnel in general"
(pp. 150–51). The great weakness of the revolution, they argue,
was the fact that it was not carried through to completion. In part
this was because of the war; in part, a consequence of the policies
of the central government. They too emphasize the refusal of the
Madrid government, in the early stages of collectivization, to
grant credits or supply funds to collectivized industry or agriculture—in the case of Catalonia, even when substantial guarantees
were offered by the Catalonian government. Thus the collectivized enterprises were forced to exist on what assets had been
seized at the time of the revolution. The control of gold and
credit "permitted the government to restrict and prevent the
function of collective enterprises at will" (p. 144).

According to Broué and Témime, it was the restriction of
credit that finally destroyed collectivized industry. The Companys
government in Catalonia refused to create a bank for industry and
credit, as demanded by the CNT and POUM, and the central
government (relying, in this case, on control of the banks by the
socialist UGT) was able to control the flow of capital and "to reserve credit for private enterprise." All attempts to obtain credit

for collectivized industry were unsuccessful, they maintain, and "the movement of collectivization was restricted, then halted, the government remaining in control of industry through the medium of the banks . . . [and later] through its control of the choice of managers and directors," who often turned out to be the former owners and managers, under new titles. The situation was similar in the case of collectivized agriculture (pp. 204 f.).

The situation was duly recognized in the West. The *New York Times,* in February 1938, observed: "The principle of State intervention and control of business and industry, as against workers' control of them in the guise of collectivization, is gradually being established in loyalist Spain by a series of decrees now appearing. Coincidentally there is to be established the principle of private ownership and the rights of corporations and companies to what is lawfully theirs under the Constitution." [84]

Morrow cites (pp. 64–65) a series of acts by the Catalonian government restricting collectivization, once power had shifted away from the new institutions set up by the workers' revolution of July 1936. On February 3, the collectivization of the dairy trade was declared illegal. [85] In April, "the Generalidad annulled workers' control over the customs by refusing to certify workers' ownership of material that had been exported and was being tied up in foreign courts by suits of former owners; henceforth the factories and agricultural collectives exporting goods were at the mercy of the government." In May, as has already been noted, the collectivization decree of October 24 was rescinded, with the argument that the decree "was dictated without competency by the Generalidad," because "there was not, nor is there yet, legislation of the [Spanish] state to apply" and "article 44 of the Constitution declares expropriation and socialization are functions of the State." A decree of August 28 "gave the government the right to intervene in or take over any mining or metallurgical plant." The anarchist newspaper *Solidaridad Obrera* reported in October

a decision of the department of purchases of the Ministry of Defense that it would make contracts for purchases only with enterprises functioning "on the basis of their old owners" or "under
the corresponding intervention controlled by the Ministry of Finance and Economy."[86]

Returning to Jackson's statement that "In Catalonia, the CNT
factory committees dragged their heels on war production,
claiming that the government deprived them of raw materials
and was favoring the *bourgeoisie*," I believe one must conclude
that this statement is more an expression of Jackson's bias in favor
of capitalist democracy than a description of the historical facts.
At the very least, we can say this much: Jackson presents no evidence to support his conclusion; there is a factual basis for ques-
tioning it. I have cited a number of sources that the liberal
historian would regard, quite correctly, as biased in favor of the
revolution. My point is that the failure of objectivity, the deep-
seated bias of liberal historians, is a matter much less normally
taken for granted, and that there are good grounds for supposing
that this failure of objectivity has seriously distorted the judgments that are rather brashly handed down about the nature of
the Spanish revolution.

Continuing with the analysis of Jackson's judgments, unsup-
ported by any cited evidence, consider his remark, quoted above,
that in Barcelona "the naïve optimism of the revolutionary conquests of the previous August had given way to feelings of resentment and of somehow having been cheated." It is a fact that by
January 1937 there was great disaffection in Barcelona. But was
this simply a consequence of "the unsuspected complexity of
modern society"? Looking into the matter a bit more closely, we
see a rather different picture. Under Russian pressure, the PSUC
was given substantial control of the Catalonian government,
"putting into the Food Ministry [in December 1936] the man
most to the Right in present Catalan politics, Comorera"[87]—by

virtue of his political views, the most willing collaborator with the general Communist party position. According to Jackson, Comorera "immediately took steps to end barter and requisitioning, and became a defender of the peasants against the revolution" (p. 314); he "ended requisition, restored money payments, and protected the Catalan peasants against further collectivization" (p. 361). This is all that Jackson has to say about Juan Comorera.

We learn more from other sources: for example, Borkenau, who was in Barcelona for the second time in January 1937—and is universally recognized as a highly knowledgeable and expert observer, with strong anti-anarchist sentiments. According to Borkenau, Comorera represented "a political attitude which can best be compared with that of the extreme right wing of the German social-democracy. He had always regarded the fight against anarchism as the chief aim of socialist policy in Spain. . . . To his surprise, he found unexpected allies for his dislike [of anarchist policies] in the communists."[88] It was impossible to reverse collectivization of industry at that stage in the process of counterrevolution; Comorera did succeed, however, in abolishing the system by which the provisioning of Barcelona had been organized, namely, the village committees, mostly under CNT influence, which had cooperated (perhaps, Borkenau suggests, unwillingly) in delivering flour to the towns. Continuing, Borkenau describes the situation as follows:

> . . . Comorera, starting from those principles of abstract liberalism which no administration has followed during the war, but of which right-wing socialists are the last and most religious admirers, did not substitute for the chaotic bread committees a centralized administration. He restored private commerce in bread, simply and completely. There was, in January, not even a system of rationing in Barcelona. Workers were simply left to get their

bread, with wages which had hardly changed since May, at increased prices, as well as they could. In practice it meant that the
women had to form queues from four o'clock in the morning
onwards. The resentment in the working-class districts was naturally acute, the more so as the scarcity of bread rapidly increased
after Comorera had taken office.[89]

In short, the workers of Barcelona were not merely giving way to
"feelings of resentment and of somehow having been cheated"
when they learned of "the unsuspected complexity of modern
society." Rather, they had good reason to believe that they *were*
being cheated, by the old dog with the new collar.

George Orwell's observations are also highly relevant:

Everyone who has made two visits, at intervals of months, to
Barcelona during the war has remarked upon the extraordinary
changes that took place in it. And curiously enough, whether
they went there first in August and again in January, or, like my-
self, first in December and again in April, the thing they said was
always the same: that the revolutionary atmosphere had vanished.
No doubt to anyone who had been there in August, when the
blood was scarcely dry in the streets and militia were quartered in
the small hotels, Barcelona in December would have seemed
bourgeois; to me, fresh from England, it was liker to a workers'
city than anything I had conceived possible. Now [in April] the
tide had rolled back. Once again it was an ordinary city, a little
pinched and chipped by war, but with no outward sign of working-class   predominance. . . . Fat   prosperous   men,   elegant
women, and sleek cars were everywhere. . . . The officers of the
new Popular Army, a type that had scarcely existed when I left
Barcelona, swarmed in surprising numbers . . . [wearing] an elegant khaki uniform with a tight waist, like a British Army officer's
uniform, only a little more so. I do not suppose that more than
one in twenty of them had yet been to the front, but all of them
had automatic pistols strapped to their belts; we, at the front,

could not get pistols for love or money. . . . ★ A deep change had come over the town. There were two facts that were the keynote of all else. One was that the people—the civil population—had lost much of their interest in the war; the other was that the normal division of society into rich and poor, upper class and lower class, was reasserting itself.[90]

Whereas Jackson attributes the ebbing of the revolutionary tide to the discovery of the unsuspected complexity of modern society, Orwell's firsthand observations, like those of Borkenau, suggest a far simpler explanation. What calls for explanation is not the disaffection of the workers of Barcelona but the curious constructions of the historian.

Let me repeat, at this point, Jackson's comments regarding Juan Comorera: Comorera "immediately took steps to end barter and requisitioning, and became a defender of the peasants against the revolution"; he "ended requisitions, restored money payments, and protected the Catalan peasants against further collectivization." These comments imply that the peasantry of Catalonia was, as a body, opposed to the revolution and that Comorera put a stop to the collectivization that they feared. Jackson nowhere indicates any divisions among the peasantry on this issue and offers no support for the implied claim that collectivization was in process at the period of Comorera's access to power. In fact, it is questionable that Comorera's rise to power affected the course of collectivization in Catalonia. Evidence is difficult to come by, but it seems that collectivization of agriculture in Catalonia was not, in any event, extensive, and that it was not extending in December, when Comorera took office. We know from anarchist sources that there had been instances of forced collectivization in

---

★ Orwell had just returned from the Aragon front, where he had been serving with the POUM militia in an area heavily dominated by left-wing (POUM and anarchist) troops.

Catalonia,[91] but I can find no evidence that Comorera "protected the peasantry" from forced collectivization. Furthermore, it is misleading, at best, to imply that the peasantry *as a whole* was opposed to collectivization. A more accurate picture is presented by Bolloten (p. 56), who points out that "if the individual farmer viewed with dismay the swift and widespread development of collectivized agriculture, the farm workers of the Anarchosyndicalist CNT and the Socialist UGT saw in it, on the contrary, the commencement of a new era." In short, there was a complex class struggle in the countryside, though one learns little about it from Jackson's oversimplified and misleading account. It would seem fair to suppose that this distortion again reflects Jackson's antipathy towards the revolution and its goals. I will return to this question directly, with reference to areas where agricultural collectivization was much more extensive than in Catalonia.

The complexities of modern society that baffled and confounded the unsuspecting anarchist workers of Barcelona, as Jackson enumerates them, were the following: the accumulating food and supply problems and the administration of frontier posts, villages, and public utilities. As just noted, the food and supply problems seem to have accumulated most rapidly under the brilliant leadership of Juan Comorera. So far as the frontier posts are concerned, the situation, as Jackson elsewhere describes it (p. 368), was basically as follows: "In Catalonia the anarchists had, ever since July 18, controlled the customs stations at the French border. On April 17, 1937, the reorganized carabineros, acting on orders of the Finance Minister, Juan Negrín, began to reoccupy the frontier. At least eight anarchists were killed in clashes with the carabineros." Apart from this difficulty, admittedly serious, there seems little reason to suppose that the problem of manning frontier posts contributed to the ebbing of the revolutionary tide. The available records do not indicate that the problems of administering villages or public utilities were either "unsuspected" or too complex for the Catalonian workers—a remarkable and unsuspected development, but one which nevertheless appears to be borne out by the evidence available to us. I want to emphasize again that Jackson presents no evidence to support his conclusions about the ebbing of the revolutionary tide and the reasons for the disaffection of the Catalonian workers. Once again, I think it fair to attribute his conclusions to the elitist bias of the liberal intellectual rather than to the historical record.

Consider next Jackson's comment that the anarchists "explained the loss of Málaga as due in large measure to the low morale and the disorientation of the Andalusian proletariat, which saw the Valencia government evolving steadily toward the right." Again, it seems that Jackson regards this as just another indication of the naiveté and unreasonableness of the Spanish anarchists. However, here again there is more to the story. One of the primary sources that Jackson cites is Borkenau, quite naturally, since Borkenau spent several days in the area just prior to the fall of Málaga on February 8, 1937. But Borkenau's detailed observations tend to bear out the anarchist "explanation," at least in part. He believed that Málaga might have been saved, but only by a "fight of despair" with mass involvement, of a sort that "the anarchists might have led." But two factors prevented such a defense: first, the officer assigned to lead the defense, Lieutenant Colonel Villalba, "interpreted this task as a purely military one, whereas in reality he had no military means at his disposal but only the forces of a popular movement"; he was a professional officer, "who in the secrecy of his heart hated the spirit of the militia" and was incapable of comprehending the "political factor." [92] A second factor was the significant decline, by February, of political consciousness and mass involvement. The anarchist committees were no longer functioning and the authority of the police and Civil Guards had been restored. "The nuisance of hundreds of

independent village police bodies had disappeared, but with it
the passionate interest of the village in the civil war. . . . The
short interlude of the Spanish Soviet system was at an end" (p.
212). After reviewing the local situation in Málaga and the con-
flicts in the Valencia government (which failed to provide support or arms for the militia defending Málaga), Borkenau
concludes (p. 228): "The Spanish republic paid with the fall of
Málaga for the decision of the Right wing of its camp to make an
end of social revolution and of its Left wing not to allow that."
Jackson's discussion of the fall of Málaga refers to the terror and
political rivalries within the town but makes no reference to the
fact that Borkenau's description, and the accompanying interpretation, do support the belief that the defeat was due in large measure to low morale and to the incapacity, or unwillingness, of the
Valencia government to fight a popular war. On the contrary, he
concludes that Colonel Villalba's lack of means for "controlling
the bitter political rivalries" was one factor that prevented him
from carrying out the essential military tasks. Thus he seems to
adopt the view that Borkenau condemns, that the task was a
"purely military one." Borkenau's eyewitness account appears to
me much more convincing.

In this case too Jackson has described the situation in a somewhat misleading fashion, perhaps again because of the elitist bias
that dominates the liberal–Communist interpretation of the
Civil War. Like Lieutenant Colonel Villalba, liberal historians
often reveal a strong distaste for "the forces of a popular movement" and "the spirit of the militia." And an argument can be
given that they correspondingly fail to comprehend the "political factor."

In the May Days of 1937, the revolution in Catalonia received
the final blow. On May 3, the councilor for public order, PSUC
member Rodríguez Salas, appeared at the central telephone

building with a detachment of police, without prior warning or consultation with the anarchist ministers in the government, to take over the telephone exchange. The exchange, formerly the property of IT&T, had been captured by Barcelona workers in July and had since functioned under the control of a UGT-CNT committee, with a governmental delegate, quite in accord with the collectivization decree of October 24, 1936. According to the London *Daily Worker* (May 11, 1937), "Salas sent the armed republican police to disarm the employees there, most of them members of the CNT unions." The motive, according to Juan Comorera, was "to put a stop to an abnormal situation," namely, that no one could speak over the telephone "without the indiscreet ear of the controller knowing it."[93] Armed resistance in the telephone building prevented its occupation. Local defense committees erected barricades throughout Barcelona. Companys and the anarchist leaders pleaded with the workers to disarm. An uneasy truce continued until May 6, when the first detachments of Assault Guards arrived, violating the promises of the government that the truce would be observed and military forces withdrawn. The troops were under the command of General Pozas, formerly commander of the hated Civil Guard and now a member of the Communist party. In the fighting that followed, there were some five hundred killed and over a thousand wounded. "The May Days in reality sounded the death-knell of the revolution, announcing political defeat for all and death for certain of the revolutionary leaders."[94]

These events—of enormous significance in the history of the Spanish revolution—Jackson sketches in bare outline as a marginal incident. Obviously the historian's account must be selective; from the left-liberal point of view that Jackson shares with Hugh Thomas and many others, the liquidation of the revolution in Catalonia was a minor event, as the revolution itself was

merely a kind of irrelevant nuisance, a minor irritant diverting
energy from the struggle to save the bourgeois government. The
decision to crush the revolution by force is described as follows:

> On May 5, Companys obtained a fragile truce, on the basis of
> which the PSUC councilors were to retire from the regional
> government, and the question of the Telephone Company was
> left to future negotiation. That very night, however, Antonio
> Sesé, a UGT official who was about to enter the reorganized cab-
> inet, was murdered. In any event, the Valencia authorities were in
> no mood to temporize further with the Catalan Left. On May 6
> several thousand *asaltos* arrived in the city, and the Republican
> Navy demonstrated in the port.[95]

What is interesting about this description is what is left unsaid.
For example, there is no comment on the fact that the dispatch of
the *asaltos* violated the "fragile truce" that had been accepted by
the Barcelona workers and the anarchist and the POUM troops
nearby, and barely a mention of the bloody consequences or the
political meaning of this unwillingness "to temporize further
with the Catalan Left." There is no mention of the fact that along
with Sesé, Berneri and other anarchist leaders were murdered,
not only during the May Days but in the weeks preceding.[96]
Jackson does not refer to the fact that along with the Republican
navy, British ships also "demonstrated" in the port.[97] Nor does he
refer to Orwell's telling observations about the Assault Guards, as
compared to the troops at the front, where he had spent the preceding months. The Assault Guards "were splendid troops, much
the best I had seen in Spain. . . . I was used to the ragged,
scarcely-armed militia on the Aragon front, and I had not known
that the Republic possessed troops like these. . . . The Civil
Guards and Carabineros, who were not intended for the front at
all, were better armed and far better clad than ourselves. I suspect
it is the same in all wars—always the same contrast between the

sleek police in the rear and the ragged soldiers in the line." [98] (See page 79 below.)

The contrast reveals a good deal about the nature of the war, as it was understood by the Valencia government. Later, Orwell was to make this conclusion explicit: "A government which sends boys of fifteen to the front with rifles forty years old and keeps its biggest men and newest weapons in the rear is manifestly more afraid of the revolution than of the fascists. Hence the feeble war policy of the past six months, and hence the compromise with which the war will almost certainly end." [99] Jackson's account of these events, with its omissions and assumptions, suggests that he perhaps shares the view that the greatest danger in Spain would have been a victory of the revolution.

Jackson apparently discounts Orwell's testimony, to some extent, commenting that "the readers should bear in mind Orwell's own honest statement that he knew very little about the political complexities of the struggle." This is a strange comment. For one thing, Orwell's analysis of the "political complexities of the struggle" bears up rather well after thirty years; if it is defective, it is probably in his tendency to give too much prominence to the POUM in comparison with the anarchists—not surprising, in view of the fact that he was with the POUM militia. His exposure of the fatuous nonsense that was appearing at the time in the Stalinist and liberal presses appears quite accurate, and later discoveries have given little reason to challenge the basic facts that he reported or the interpretation that he proposed in the heat of the conflict. Orwell does, in fact, refer to his own "political ignorance." Commenting on the final defeat of the revolution in May, he states: "I realized—though owing to my political ignorance, not so clearly as I ought to have done—that when the Government felt more sure of itself there would be reprisals." But this form of "political ignorance" has simply been compounded in more recent historical work.

Shortly after the May Days, the Caballero government fell and Juan Negrín became premier of Republican Spain. Negrín is described as follows, by Broué and Témime: ". . . he is an unconditional defender of capitalist property and resolute adversary of collectivization, whom the CNT ministers find blocking all of their proposals. He is the one who solidly reorganized the carabineros and presided over the transfer of the gold reserves of the Republic to the USSR. He enjoyed the confidence of the moderates . . . [and] was on excellent terms with the Communists."

The first major act of the Negrín government was the suppression of the POUM and the consolidation of central control over Catalonia. The government next turned to Aragon, which had been under largely anarchist control since the first days of the revolution, and where agricultural collectivization was quite extensive and Communist elements very weak. The municipal councils of Aragon were coordinated by the Council of Aragon, headed by Joaquín Ascaso, a well-known CNT militant, one of whose brothers had been killed during the May Days. Under the Caballero government, the anarchists had agreed to give representation to other antifascist parties, including the Communists, but the majority remained anarchist. In August the Negrín government announced the dissolution of the Council of Aragon and dispatched a division of the Spanish army, commanded by the Communist officer Enrique Lister, to enforce the dissolution of the local committees, dismantle the collectives, and establish central government control. Ascaso was arrested on the charge of having been responsible for the robbery of jewelry—namely, the jewelry "robbed" by the Council for its own use in the fall of 1936. The local anarchist press was suppressed in favor of a Communist journal, and in general local anarchist centers were forcefully occupied and closed. The last anarchist stronghold was captured, with tanks and artillery, on September 21. Because of government-imposed censorship, there is very little of a direct record of these events, and the major histories pass over them quickly.[100] According to Morrow, "the official CNT press . . . compared the assault on Aragon with the subjection of Asturias by Lopez Ochoa in October 1934"—the latter, one of the bloodiest acts of repression in modern Spanish history. Although this is an exaggeration, it is a fact that the popular organs of administration were wiped out by Lister's legions, and the revolution was now over, so far as Aragon was concerned.

About these events, Jackson has the following comments:

> On August 11 the government announced the dissolution of the *Consejo de Aragón*, the anarchist-dominated administration which had been recognized by Largo Caballero in December, 1936. The peasants were known to hate the Consejo, the anarchists had deserted the front during the Barcelona fighting, and the very existence of the Consejo was a standing challenge to the authority of the central government. For all these reasons Negrín did not hesitate to send in troops, and to arrest the anarchist officials. Once their authority had been broken, however, they were released.[101]

These remarks are most interesting. Consider first the charge that the anarchists had deserted the front during the May Days. It is true that elements of certain anarchist and POUM divisions were prepared to march on Barcelona, but after the "fragile truce" was established on May 5, they did not do so; no anarchist forces even approached Barcelona to defend the Barcelona proletariat and its institutions from attack. However, a motorized column of 5,000 Assault Guards was sent from the front by the government to break the "fragile truce."[102] Hence the only forces to "desert the front" during the Barcelona fighting were those dispatched by the government to complete the job of dismantling the revolution, by force. Recall Orwell's observations quoted above, pages 76–77.

What about Jackson's statement that "the peasants were known to hate the Consejo"? As in the other cases I have cited, Jackson gives no indication of any evidence on which such a judgment might be based. The most detailed investigation of the collectives is from anarchist sources, and they indicate that Aragon was one of the areas where collectivization was most widespread and successful.[103] Both the CNT and the UGT Land Workers' Federation were vigorous in their support for collectivization, and there is no doubt that both were mass organizations. A number of nonanarchists, observing collectivization in Aragon firsthand, gave very favorable reports and stressed the voluntary character of collectivization.[104] According to Gaston Leval, an anarchist observer who carried out detailed investigation of rural collectivization, "in Aragon 75 percent of small proprietors have voluntarily adhered to the new order of things," and others were not forced to involve themselves in collectives.[105] Other anarchist observers—Augustin Souchy in particular—gave detailed observations of the functioning of the Aragon collectives. Unless one is willing to assume a fantastic degree of falsification, it is impossible to reconcile their descriptions with the claim that "the peasants were known to hate the Consejo"— unless, of course, one restricts the term "peasant" to "individual farm owner," in which case it might very well be true, but would justify disbanding the Council only on the assumption that the rights of the individual farm owner must predominate, not those of the landless worker. There is little doubt that the collectives were economically successful,[106] hardly likely if collectivization were forced and hated by the peasantry.

I have already cited Bolloten's general conclusion, based on very extensive documentary evidence, that while the individual farmer may have viewed the development of collectivized agriculture with dismay, "the farm workers of the Anarchosyndicalist CNT and the Socialist UGT saw in it, on the contrary, the commencement of a new era." This conclusion seems quite reasonable, on the basis of the materials that are available. With respect to Aragon, specifically, he remarks that the "debt-ridden peasants were strongly affected by the ideas of the CNT and FAI, a factor that gave a powerful spontaneous impulse to collective farming," though difficulties are cited by anarchist sources, which in general appear to be quite honest about failures. Bolloten cites two Communist sources, among others, to the effect that about 70 percent of the population in rural areas of Aragon lived in collectives (p. 71); he adds that "many of the region's 450 collectives were largely voluntary," although "the presence of militiamen from the neighbouring region of Catalonia, the immense majority of whom were members of the CNT and FAI" was "in some measure" responsible for the extensive collectivization. He also points out that in many instances peasant proprietors who were not compelled to adhere to the collective system did so for other reasons: ". . . not only were they prevented from employing hired labour and disposing freely of their crops . . . but they were often denied all benefits enjoyed by members" (p. 72). Bolloten cites the attempt of the Communists in April 1937 to cause dissension in "areas where the CNT and UGT had established collective farms by mutual agreement" (p. 195), leading in some cases to pitched battles and dozens of assassinations, according to CNT sources.[107]

Bolloten's detailed analysis of the events of the summer of 1937 sheds considerable light on the question of peasant attitudes towards collectivization in Aragon:

> It was inevitable that the attacks on the collectives should have had an unfavorable effect upon rural economy and upon morale, for while it is true that in some areas collectivization was anathema to the majority of peasants, it is no less true that in others collective farms were organized spontaneously by the bulk of the

peasant population. In Toledo province, for example, where even before the war rural collectives existed, 83 per cent of the peasants, according to a source friendly to the Communists, decided in favour of the collective cultivation of the soil. As the campaign against the collective farms reached its height just before the summer harvest [1937] . . . a pall of dismay and apprehension descended upon the agricultural labourers. Work in the fields was abandoned in many places or only carried on apathetically, and there was danger that a substantial portion of the harvest, vital for the war effort, would be left to rot. [P. 196]

It was under these circumstances, he points out, that the Communists were forced to change their policy and—temporarily—to tolerate the collectives. A decree was passed legalizing collectives *"during the current agricultural year"* (his italics) and offering them some aid. This "produced a sense of relief in the countryside during the vital period of the harvest." Immediately after the crops had been gathered, the policy changed again to one of harsh repression. Bolloten cites Communist sources to the effect that "a short though fierce campaign at the beginning of August" prepared the way for the dissolution of the Council of Aragon. Following the dissolution decree, "the newly appointed Governor General, José Ignacio Mantecón, a member of the Left Republican Party, but a secret Communist sympathizer [who joined the party in exile, after the war], . . . ordered the break-up of the collective farms." The means: Lister's division, which restored the old order by force and terror. Bolloten cites Communist sources conceding the excessive harshness of Lister's methods. He quotes the Communist general secretary of the Institute of Agrarian Reform, who admits that the measures taken to dissolve the collectives were "a very grave mistake, and produced tremendous disorganization in the countryside," as "those persons who were discontented with the collectives . . . took them by assault, carrying away and dividing up the harvest and farm implements without respecting the collectives that had been formed without violence or pressure, that were prosperous, and that were a model of organization. . . . As a result, labour in the fields was suspended almost entirely, and a quarter of the land had not been prepared at the time for sowing" (p. 200). Once again, it was necessary to ameliorate the harsh repression of the collectives, to prevent disaster. Summarizing these events, Bolloten describes the resulting situation as follows:

> But although the situation in Aragon improved in some degree, the hatreds and resentments generated by the break-up of the collectives and by the repression that followed were never wholly dispelled. Nor was the resultant disillusionment that sapped the spirit of the Anarchosyndicalist forces on the Aragon front ever entirely removed, a disillusionment that no doubt contributed to the collapse of that front a few months later. . . . after the destruction of the collective farms in Aragon, the Communist Party was compelled to modify its policy, and support collectives also in other regions against former owners who sought the return of confiscated land. . . . [Pp. 200–201]

Returning to Jackson's remarks, I think we must conclude that they seriously misrepresent the situation.[108] The dissolution of the Council of Aragon and the large-scale destruction of the collectives by military force was simply another stage in the eradication of the popular revolution and the restoration of the old order. Let me emphasize that I am not criticizing Jackson for his negative attitude towards the social revolution, but rather for the failure of objectivity when he deals with the revolution and the ensuing repression.

Among historians of the Spanish Civil War, the dominant view is that the Communist policy was in essentials the correct one—that in order to consolidate domestic and international support for the Republic it was necessary to block and then reverse the social revolution. Jackson, for example, states that Caballero "realized that it was absolutely necessary to rebuild the authority of the Republican state and to work in close cooperation with the middle-class liberals." The anarchist leaders who entered the government shared this view, putting their trust in the good faith of liberals such as Companys and believing—naively, as events were to show—that the Western democracies would come to their aid.

A policy diametrically opposed to this was advocated by Camillo Berneri. In his open letter to the anarchist minister Federica Montseny[109] he summarizes his views in the following way: "The dilemma, war or revolution, no longer has meaning. *The only dilemma is this: either victory over Franco through revolutionary war, or defeat*" (his italics). He argued that Morocco should be granted independence and that an attempt should be made to stir up rebellion throughout North Africa. Thus a revolutionary struggle should be undertaken against Western capitalism in North Africa and, simultaneously, against the bourgeois regime in Spain, which was gradually dismantling the accomplishments of the July revolution. The primary front should be political. Franco relied heavily on Moorish contingents, including a substantial number from French Morocco. The Republic might exploit this fact, demoralizing the Nationalist forces and perhaps even winning them to the revolutionary cause by political agitation based on the concrete alternative of pan-Islamic—specifically, Moroccan—revolution. Writing in April 1937, Berneri urged that the army of the Republic be reorganized for the defense of the revolution, so that it might recover the spirit of popular participation of the early days of the revolution. He quotes the words of his compatriot Louis Bertoni, writing from the Huesca front:

The Spanish war, deprived of all new faith, of any idea of a social transformation, of all revolutionary grandeur, of any universal meaning, is now merely a national war of independence that must be carried on to avoid the extermination that the international plutocracy demands. There remains a terrible question of life or death, but no longer a war to build a new society and a new humanity.

In such a war, the human element that might bring victory over fascism is lost.

In retrospect, Berneri's ideas seem quite reasonable. Delegations of Moroccan nationalists did in fact approach the Valencia government asking for arms and matériel, but were refused by Caballero, who actually proposed territorial concessions in North Africa to France and England to try to win their support. Commenting on these facts, Broué and Témime observe that these policies deprived the Republic of "the instrument of revolutionary defeatism in the enemy army," and even of a possible weapon against Italian intervention. Jackson, on the other hand, dismisses Berneri's suggestion with the remark that independence for Morocco (as for that matter, even aid to the Moroccan nationalists) was "a gesture that would have been highly appreciated in Paris and London." Of course it is correct that France and Britain would hardly have appreciated this development. As Berneri points out, "it goes without saying that one cannot simultaneously guarantee French and British interests in Morocco and carry out an insurrection." But Jackson's comment does not touch on the central issue, namely, whether the Spanish revolution could have been preserved, both from the fascists at the front and from the bourgeois-Communist coalition within the Republic, by a revolutionary war of the sort that the left proposed— or, for that matter, whether the Republic might not have been saved by a political struggle that involved Franco's invading

Moorish troops, or at least eroded their morale. It is easy to see why Caballero was not attracted by this bold scheme, given his reliance on the eventual backing of the Western democracies. On the basis of what we know today, however, Jackson's summary dismissal of revolutionary war is much too abrupt.

Furthermore, Bertoni's observations from the Huesca front are borne out by much other evidence, some of it cited earlier. Even those who accepted the Communist strategy of discipline and central control as necessary concede that the repressions that formed an ineliminable part of this strategy "tended to break the fighting spirit of the people."[110] One can only speculate, but it seems to me that many commentators have seriously underestimated the significance of the political factor, the potential strength of a popular struggle to defend the achievements of the revolution. It is perhaps relevant that Asturias, the one area of Spain where the system of CNT-UGT committees was not eliminated in favor of central control, is also the one area where guerrilla warfare continued well after Franco's victory. Broué and Témime observe[111] that the resistance of the partisans of Asturias "demonstrates the depth of the revolutionary élan, which had not been shattered by the reinstitution of state authority, conducted here with greater prudence." There can be no doubt that the revolution was both widespread and deeply rooted in the Spanish masses. It seems quite possible that a revolutionary war of the sort advocated by Berneri would have been successful, despite the greater military force of the fascist armies. The idea that men can overcome machines no longer seems as romantic or naive as it may have a few years ago.

Furthermore, the trust placed in the bourgeois government by the anarchist leaders was not honored, as the history of the counterrevolution clearly shows. In retrospect, it seems that Berneri was correct in arguing that they should not have taken part in the bourgeois government, but should rather have sought to replace this government with the institutions created by the revolution.[112] The anarchist minister Garcia Oliver stated that "we had confidence in the word and in the person of a Catalan democrat and retained and supported Companys as President of the Generalitat,"[113] at a time when in Catalonia, at least, the workers' organizations could easily have replaced the state apparatus and dispensed with the former political parties, as they had replaced the old economy with an entirely new structure. Companys recognized fully that there were limits beyond which he could not cooperate with the anarchists. In an interview with H. E. Kaminski, he refused to specify these limits, but merely expressed his hope that "the anarchist masses will not oppose the good sense of their leaders," who have "accepted the responsibilities incumbent upon them"; he saw his task as "directing these responsibilities in the proper path," not further specified in the interview, but shown by the events leading up to the May Days.[114] Probably, Companys' attitude towards this willingness of the anarchist leaders to cooperate was expressed accurately in his reaction to the suggestion of a correspondent of the *New Statesman and Nation,* who predicted that the assassination of the anarchist mayor of Puigcerdá would lead to a revolt: "[Companys] laughed scornfully and said the anarchists would capitulate as they always had before."[115] As has already been pointed out in some detail, the liberal-Communist Party coalition had no intention of letting the war against Franco take precedence over the crushing of the revolution. A spokesman for Comorera put the matter clearly: "This slogan has been attributed to the P.S.U.C.: 'Before taking Saragossa, it is necessary to take Barcelona.' This reflects the situation exactly. . . ."[116] Comorera himself had, from the beginning, pressed Companys to resist the CNT.[117] The first task of the antifascist coalition, he maintained, was to dissolve the revolutionary committees.[118] I have already cited a good deal of evidence indicating that the repression conducted by the Popular Front seriously weakened popular commitment and involvement in the antifascist war. What was evident to George Orwell was also clear to the Barcelona workers and the peasants in the collectivized villages of Aragon: the liberal-Communist coalition would not tolerate a revolutionary transformation of Spanish society; it would commit itself fully to the anti-Franco struggle only after the old order was firmly re-established, by force, if necessary.[119]

There is little doubt that farm workers in the collectives understood quite well the social content of the drive towards consolidation and central control. We learn this not only from anarchist sources but also from the socialist press in the spring of 1937. On May 1, the Socialist party newspaper *Adelante* had the following to say:

> At the outbreak of the Fascist revolt the labor organizations and the democratic elements in the country were in agreement that the so-called Nationalist Revolution, which threatened to plunge our people into an abyss of deepest misery, could be halted only by a Social Revolution. The Communist Party, however, opposed this view with all its might. It had apparently completely forgotten its old theories of a "workers' and peasants' republic" and a "dictatorship of the proletariat." From its constant repetition of its new slogan of the parliamentary democratic republic it is clear that it has lost all sense of reality. When the Catholic and conservative sections of the Spanish bourgeoisie saw their old system smashed and could find no way out, the Communist Party instilled new hope into them. It assured them that the democratic bourgeois republic for which it was pleading put no obstacles in the way of Catholic propaganda and, above all, that it stood ready to defend the class interests of the bourgeoisie.[120]

That this realization was widespread in the rural areas was underscored dramatically by a questionnaire sent by *Adelante* to secretaries of the UGT Federation of Land Workers, published in June 1937.[121] The results are summarized as follows:

> The replies to these questions revealed an astounding unanimity. Everywhere the same story. The peasant collectives are today most vigorously opposed by the Communist Party. The Communists organize the well-to-do farmers who are on the lookout for cheap labor and are, for this reason, outspokenly hostile to the cooperative undertakings of the poor peasants.
>
> It is the element which before the revolution sympathized with the Fascists and Monarchists which, according to the testimony of the trade-union representatives, is now flocking into the ranks of the Communist Party. As to the general effect of Communist activity on the country, the secretaries of the U.G.T. had only one opinion, which the representative of the Valencia organization put in these words: "It is a misfortune in the fullest sense of the word."[122]

It is not difficult to imagine how the recognition of this "misfortune" must have affected the willingness of the land workers to take part in the antifascist war, with all the sacrifices that this entailed.

The attitude of the central government to the revolution was brutally revealed by its acts and is attested as well in its propaganda. A former minister describes the situation as follows:

> The fact that is concealed by the coalition of the Spanish Communist Party with the left Republicans and right wing Socialists is that there has been a successful social revolution in half of Spain. Successful, that is, in the collectivization of factories and farms which are operated under trade union control, and operated quite efficiently. During the three months that I was director of propaganda for the United States and England under Alvarez del Vayo, then Foreign Minister for the Valencia Government, I was instructed not to send out one word about this revolution in

the economic system of loyalist Spain. Nor are any foreign corre-
spondents in Valencia permitted to write freely of the revolution
that has taken place.[123]

In short, there is much reason to believe that the will to fight
Franco was significantly diminished, perhaps destroyed, by the
policy of authoritarian centralization undertaken by the liberal-
Communist coalition, carried through by force, and disguised in
the propaganda that was disseminated among Western intellectuals[124] and that still dominates the writing of history. To the extent
that this is a correct judgment, the alternative proposed by
Berneri and the left "extremists" gains in plausibility.

As noted earlier, Caballero and the anarchist ministers accepted the policy of counterrevolution because of their trust in
the Western democracies, which they felt sure would sooner or
later come to their aid. This feeling was perhaps understandable
in 1937. It is strange, however, that a historian writing in the
1960s should dismiss the proposal to strike at Franco's rear by extending the revolutionary war to Morocco, on grounds that this
would have displeased Western capitalism (see page 85 above).

Berneri was quite right in his belief that the Western democracies would not take part in an antifascist struggle in Spain. In
fact, their complicity in the fascist insurrection was not slight.
French bankers, who were generally pro-Franco, blocked the release of Spanish gold to the loyalist government, thus hindering
the purchase of arms and, incidentally, increasing the reliance of
the Republic on the Soviet Union.[125] The policy of "nonintervention," which effectively blocked Western aid for the loyalist
government while Hitler and Mussolini in effect won the war for
Franco, was also technically initiated by the French government—though apparently under heavy British pressure.[126]

As far as Great Britain is concerned, the hope that it would
come to the aid of the Republic was always unrealistic. A few

days after the Franco coup, the foreign editor of *Paris-Soir* wrote: "At least four countries are already taking active interest in the battle—France, which is supporting the Madrid Government, and Britain, Germany and Italy, each of which is giving discreet but nevertheless effective assistance to one group or another among the insurgents." [127] In fact, British support for Franco took a fairly concrete form at the very earliest stages of the insurrection. The Spanish navy remained loyal to the Republic,* and made some attempt to prevent Franco from ferrying troops from Morocco to Spain. Italian and German involvement in overcoming these efforts is well documented;[128] the British role has received less attention, but can be determined from contemporary reports. On August 11, 1936, the *New York Times* carried a front-page report on British naval actions in the Straits of Gibraltar, commenting that "this action helps the Rebels by preventing attacks on Algeciras, where troops from Morocco land." (A few days earlier, loyalist warships had bombarded Algeciras, damaging the British consulate.) An accompanying dispatch from Gibraltar describes the situation as it appeared from there:

> Angered by the Spanish factions' endangering of shipping and neutral Gibraltar territory in their fighting, Great Britain virtually blockaded Gibraltar Harbor last night with the huge battleship Queen Elizabeth in the center of the entrance, constantly playing searchlights on near-by waters.
>
> Many British warships patrolled the entire Strait today, determined to prevent interference with Britain's control over the entrance to the Mediterranean, a vital place in the British "lifeline to the East."
>
> This action followed repeated warnings to the Spanish Government and yesterday's decree that no more fighting would be

---

* To be more precise, pro-Franco officers were killed, and the seamen remained loyal to the Republic, in many instances.

permitted in Gibraltar Harbor. The British at Gibraltar had become increasingly nervous after the shelling of Algeciras by the Loyalist battleship Jaime I.

Although British neutrality is still maintained, the patrol of the Strait and the closing of the harbor will aid the military Rebels because Loyalist warships cannot attempt to take Algeciras, now in Rebel hands, and completely isolate the Rebels from Morocco. The Rebels now can release some troops, who were rushed back to Algeciras, for duty further north in the drive for Madrid.

It was reported in Gibraltar tonight that the Rebels had sent a transport across the Strait and had landed more troops from Morocco for use in the columns that are marching northward from headquarters at Seville.

This was the second time this year that Britain warned a power when she believed her measure of Mediterranean control was threatened, and it remains to be seen whether the Madrid Government will flout the British as the Italians did. If it attempts to do so, the British gunners of the Gibraltar fort have authority to fire warning shots. What will happen if such shots go unheeded is obvious.

All the British here refer to the Madrid Government as the "Communists" and there is no doubt where British sympathies now lie, encouraged by the statement of General Francisco Franco, leader of the Rebels, that he is not especially cooperating with Italy.

The British Government has ordered Spaniards here to cease plotting or be expelled and has asked Britons "loyally to refrain from either acting or speaking publicly in such a manner as to display marked partiality or partisanship."

The warning, issued in the official Gibraltar Gazette, was signed by the British Colonial Secretary here.

The warning was issued after reports of possible Communist troubles here had reached official ears and after strong complaints that Spanish Rebels were in Gibraltar. It was said Rebels were making headquarters here and entering La Linea to fight. [Italics mine]

I have quoted this dispatch in full because it conveys rather accurately the character of British "neutrality" in the early stages of the war and thenceforth. In May 1938, the British ambassador to Spain, Sir Henry Chilton, "expressed the conviction that a Franco victory was necessary for peace in Spain; that there was not the slightest chance that Italy and/or Germany would dominate Spain; and that even if it were possible for the Spanish Government to win (which he did not believe) he was convinced that a victory for Franco would be better for Great Britain." [129] Churchill, who was at first violently opposed to the Republic, modified his position somewhat after the crushing of the revolution in the summer of 1937. What particularly pleased him was the forceful repression of the anarchists and the militarization of the Republic (necessary when "the entire structure of civilization and social life is destroyed," as it had been by the revolution, now happily subdued). [130] However, his good feelings towards the Republic remained qualified. In an interview of August 14, 1938, he expressed himself as follows: "Franco has all the right on his side because he loves his country. Also Franco is defending Europe against the Communist danger—if you wish to put it in those terms. But I, I am English, and I prefer the triumph of the wrong cause. I prefer that the other side wins, because Franco could be an upset or a threat to British interests, and the others no." [131]

The Germans were quite aware of British sentiments, naturally, and therefore were much concerned that the supervisory committee for the nonintervention agreement be located in London rather than Paris. The German Foreign Ministry official responsible for this matter expressed his view on August 29,

1936, as follows: "Naturally, we have to count on complaints of all kinds being brought up in London regarding failure to observe the obligation not to intervene, but we cannot avoid such complaints in any case. It can, in fact, only be agreeable to us if the center of gravity, which after all has thus far been in Paris because of the French initiative, is transferred to London."[132] They were not disappointed. In November, Foreign Secretary Anthony Eden stated in the House of Commons: "So far as breaches [of the nonintervention agreement] are concerned, I wish to state categorically that I think there are other Governments more to blame than those of Germany and Italy."[133] There was no factual basis for this statement, but it did reflect British attitudes. It is interesting that according to German sources, England was at that time supplying Franco with munitions through Gibraltar and, at the same time, providing information to Germany about Russian arms deliveries to the Republic.[134]

The British left was for the most part in support of the liberal-Communist coalition, regarding Caballero as an "infantile leftist" and the anarchists as generally unspeakable.

The British policy of mild support for Franco was to be successful in preserving British interests in Spain, as the Germans soon discovered. A German Foreign Ministry note of October 1937 to the embassy in Nationalist Spain included the following observation: "That England cannot permanently be kept from the Spanish market as in the past is a fact with which we have to reckon. England's old relations with the Spanish mines and the Generalissimo's desire, based on political and economic considerations, to come to an understanding with England place certain limits on our chances of reserving Spanish raw materials to ourselves permanently."[135]

One can only speculate as to what might have been the effects of British support for the Republic. A discussion of this matter would take us far afield, into a consideration of British diplomacy during the late 1930s. It is perhaps worth mention, now that the "Munich analogy" is being bandied about in utter disregard for the historical facts by Secretary Rusk and a number of his academic supporters, that "containment of Communism" was not a policy invented by George Kennan in 1947. Specifically, it was a dominant theme in the diplomacy of the 1930s. In 1934, Lloyd George stated that "in a very short time, perhaps in a year, perhaps in two, the conservative elements in this country will be looking to Germany as the bulwark against Communism in Europe. . . . Do not let us be in a hurry to condemn Germany. We shall be welcoming Germany as our friend." [136] In September 1938, the Munich agreement was concluded; shortly after, both France and Britain did welcome Germany as "our friend." As noted earlier (see note 99), even Churchill's role at this time is subject to some question. Of course, the Munich agreement was the death knell for the Spanish Republic, exactly as the necessity to rely on the Soviet Union signaled the end of the Spanish revolution in 1937.

The United States, like France, exhibited less initiative in these events than Great Britain, which had far more substantial economic interests in Spain and was more of an independent force in European affairs. Nevertheless, the American record is hardly one to inspire pride. Technically, the United States adhered to a position of strict neutrality. However, a careful look raises some doubts. According to information obtained by Jackson, "the American colonel who headed the Telephone Company had placed private lines at the disposal of the Madrid plotters for their conversations with Generals Mola and Franco," [137] just prior to the insurrection on July 17. In August, the American government urged the Martin Aircraft Company not to honor an agreement made prior to the insurrection to supply aircraft to the Republic, and it also pressured the Mexican government not to reship to Spain war materials purchased in the United

States.[138] An American arms exporter, Robert Cuse, insisted on his legal right to ship airplanes and aircraft engines to the Republic in December 1936, and the State Department was forced to grant authorization. Cuse was denounced by Roosevelt as unpatriotic, though Roosevelt was forced to admit that the request was quite legal. Roosevelt contrasted the attitude of other businessmen to Cuse as follows:

> Well, these companies went along with the request of the Government. There is the 90 percent of business that is honest, I mean ethically honest. There is the 90 percent we are always pointing at with pride. And then one man does what amounts to a perfectly legal but thoroughly unpatriotic act. He represents the 10 percent of business that does not live up to the best standards. Excuse the homily, but I feel quite deeply about it.[139]

Among the businesses that remained "ethically honest" and therefore did not incur Roosevelt's wrath was the Texaco Oil Company, which violated its contracts with the Spanish Republic and shipped oil instead to Franco. (Five tankers that were on the high seas in July 1936 were diverted to Franco, who received six million dollars worth of oil on credit during the Civil War.) Apparently, neither the press nor the American government was able to discover this fact, though it was reported in left-wing journals at the time.[140] There is evidence that the American government shared the fears of Churchill and others about the dangerous forces on the Republican side. Secretary of State Cordell Hull, for example, informed Roosevelt on July 23, 1936, that "one of the most serious factors in this situation lies in the fact that the [Spanish] Government has distributed large quantities of arms and ammunition into the hands of irresponsible members of left-wing political organizations."[141]

Like Churchill, many responsible Americans began to rethink

their attitude towards the Republic after the social revolution had been crushed.[142] However, relations with Franco continued cordial. In 1957, President Eisenhower congratulated Franco on the "happy anniversary" of his rebellion,[143] and Secretary Rusk added his tribute in 1961. Upon criticism, Rusk was defended by the American ambassador to Madrid, who observed that Spain is "a nation which understands the implacable nature of the communist threat,"[144] like Thailand, South Korea, Taiwan, and selected other countries of the Free World.[145]

In the light of such facts as these, it seems to me that Jackson is not treating the historical record seriously when he dismisses the proposals of the Spanish left as absurd. Quite possibly Berneri's strategy would have failed, as did that of the liberal-Communist coalition that took over the Republic. It was far from senseless, however. I think that the failure of historians to consider it more seriously follows, once again, from the elitist bias that dominates the writing of history—and, in this case, from a certain sentimentality about the Western democracies.

The study of collectivization published by the CNT in 1937[146] concludes with a description of the village of Membrilla. "In its miserable huts live the poor inhabitants of a poor province; eight thousand people, but the streets are not paved, the town has no newspaper, no cinema, neither a café nor a library. On the other hand, it has many churches that have been burned." Immediately after the Franco insurrection, the land was expropriated and village life collectivized. "Food, clothing, and tools were distributed equitably to the whole population. Money was abolished, work collectivized, all goods passed to the community, consumption was socialized. It was, however, not a socialization of wealth but of poverty." Work continued as before. An elected council appointed committees to organize the life of the commune and its relations to the outside world. The necessities of life were distributed freely, insofar as they were available. A large

number of refugees were accommodated. A small library was established, and a small school of design.

The document closes with these words:

> The whole population lived as in a large family; functionaries,
> delegates, the secretary of the syndicates, the members of the mu-
> nicipal council, all elected, acted as heads of a family. But they
> were controlled, because special privilege or corruption would
> not be tolerated. Membrilla is perhaps the poorest village of
> Spain, but it is the most just.

An account such as this, with its concern for human relations and
the ideal of a just society, must appear very strange to the consciousness of the sophisticated intellectual, and it is therefore
treated with scorn, or taken to be naive or primitive or otherwise
irrational. Only when such prejudice is abandoned will it be possible for historians to undertake a serious study of the popular
movement that transformed Republican Spain in one of the
most remarkable social revolutions that history records.

Franz Borkenau, in commenting on the demoralization
caused by the authoritarian practices of the central government,
observes (p. 295) that "newspapers are written by Europeanized
editors, and the popular movement is inarticulate as to its deepest
impulses . . . [which are shown only] . . . by acts." The objectivity of scholarship will remain a delusion as long as these inarticulate impulses remain beyond its grasp. As far as the Spanish
revolution is concerned, its history is yet to be written.

I have concentrated on one theme—the interpretation of the
social revolution in Spain—in one work of history, a work that is
an excellent example of liberal scholarship. It seems to me that
there is more than enough evidence to show that a deep bias
against social revolution and a commitment to the values and social order of liberal bourgeois democracy has led the author to

misrepresent crucial events and to overlook major historical currents. My intention has not been to bring into question the commitment to these values—that is another matter entirely. Rather, it has been to show how this commitment has led to a striking failure of objectivity, providing an example of "counterrevolutionary subordination" of a much more subtle and interesting sort—and ultimately, I believe, a far more important one—than those discussed in the first part of this essay.

III

In opening this discussion of the Spanish revolution I referred to the classical left-wing critique of the social role of intellectuals, Marxist or otherwise, in modern society, and to Luxemburg's reservations regarding Bolshevism. Western sociologists have repeatedly emphasized the relevance of this analysis to developments in the Soviet Union,[147] with much justice. The same sociologists formulate "the world revolution of the epoch" in the following terms: "The major transformation is the decline of business (and of earlier social formations) and the rise of intellectuals and semi-intellectuals to effective power."[148] The "ultraleft" critic foresaw in these developments a new attack on human freedom and a more efficient system of exploitation. The Western sociologist sees in the rise of intellectuals to effective power the hope for a more humane and smoothly functioning society, in which problems can be solved by "piecemeal technology." Who has the sharper eye? At least this much is plain: there are dangerous tendencies in the ideology of the welfare state intelligentsia who claim to possess the technique and understanding required to manage our "postindustrial society" and to organize an international society dominated by American superpower. Many of these dangers are revealed, at a purely ideological level, in the study of the counterrevolutionary subordination of scholarship. The dangers exist both insofar as the claim to knowledge is real and insofar as it is fraudulent. Insofar as the technique of management and control exists, it can be used to consolidate the authority of those who exercise it and to diminish spontaneous and free experimentation with new social forms, as it can limit the possibilities for reconstruction of society in the interests of those who are now, to a greater or lesser extent, dispossessed. Where the techniques fail, they will be supplemented by all of the methods of coercion that modern technology provides, to preserve order and stability.

For a glimpse of what may lie ahead, consider the Godkin lectures of McGeorge Bundy, recently delivered at Harvard.[149]

Bundy urges that more power be concentrated in the executive branch of the government, now "dangerously weak in relation to its present tasks." That the powerful executive will act with justice and wisdom—this presumably needs no argument. As an example of the superior executive who should be attracted to government and given still greater power, Bundy cites Robert McNamara. Nothing could reveal more clearly the dangers inherent in the "new society" than the role that McNamara's Pentagon has played for the past half-dozen years. No doubt McNamara succeeded in doing with utmost efficiency that which should not be done at all. No doubt he has shown an unparalleled mastery of the logistics of coercion and repression, combined with the most astonishing inability to comprehend political and human factors. The efficiency of the Pentagon is no less remarkable than its pratfalls.[150] When understanding fails, there is always more force in reserve. As the "experiments in material and human resources control" collapse and "revolutionary development" grinds to a halt, we simply resort more openly to the Gestapo tactics that are barely concealed behind the façade of "pacification."[151] When American cities explode, we can expect the same. The technique of "limited warfare" translates neatly into a system of domestic repression—far more humane, as will quickly be explained, than massacring those who are unwilling to wait for the inevitable victory of the war on poverty.

Why should a liberal intellectual be so persuaded of the virtues of a political system of four-year dictatorship? The answer seems all too plain.

NOTES

1. "Politics and the Morality of Scholarship," in Max Black, ed., *The Morality of Scholarship* (Ithaca, N.Y., Cornell University Press, 1967), pp. 59–88.

2. "The War and Its Effects—II," *Congressional Record,* December 13, 1967.

3. *Congressional Record,* July 27, 1967.

4. William A. Nighswonger, *Rural Pacification in Vietnam* (Praeger Special Studies; New York, Frederick A. Praeger, Inc., 1967)—one of a series of "specialized research monographs in U.S. and international economics and politics."

5. Ithiel de Sola Pool, "The Necessity for Social Scientists Doing Research for Governments," *Background,* Vol. 10 (August 1966), p. 111.

6. Max Ways writes in *Fortune* that "McNamara, his systems analysts, and their computers are not only contributing to the practical effectiveness of U.S. action, but *raising the moral level of policy* by a more conscious and selective attention to the definition of its aims" (italics mine). Cited by Andrew Kopkind, "The Future-Planners," *New Republic,* February 25, 1967, p. 23. Comment would be superfluous.

7. Daniel Bell, "Notes on the Post-Industrial Society: Part I," *The Public Interest,* No. 6, 1967, pp. 24–35.

8. Some of the dangers are noted by Richard Goodwin, in a review of Thomas Schelling's *Arms and Influence* in the *New Yorker,* February 17, 1968, pp. 127–34. He observes that "the most profound objection to this kind of strategic theory is not its limited usefulness but its danger, for it can lead us to believe we have an understanding of events and a control over their flow which we do not have." A still more profound objection, I think, is that the pretended objectivity of "strategic theory" can be used to justify the attempt to control the flow of events.

9. Seymour M. Lipset, *Political Man* (Garden City, N.Y., Doubleday & Company, Inc., 1960), p. 406.

10. "Status Politics and New Anxieties," in *The End of Ideology* (New York, The Free Press, 1960), p. 119.

11. "The Necessity and Difficulty of Planning the Future Society," address given at the American Institute of Planners Conference, Washington, D.C., October 3, 1967. Citing this, Senator Fulbright (*op. cit.*) comments aptly that "poverty, which is a tragedy in a poor country, blights our affluent society with something more than tragedy; being unnecessary, it is deeply immoral as well." He also compares "the $904 billion we have spent on military power since World War II" with "the $96 billion we have spent, out of our regular national budget, on education, health, welfare housing, and community development." In his *Challenge to Affluence* (New York, Pantheon Books, 1963), Myrdal concludes that "In society at large there is more equality of opportunity today than there ever was. But for the bottom layer there is less or none" (p. 38). He questions the assumption that "America is still the free and open society of its cherished image and well-established ideals" and remarks that "as less and less work is required of the type that people in the urban and rural slums can offer, they will be increasingly isolated and exposed to unemployment and plain exploitation. There is an ugly smell rising from the basement of the stately American mansion" (p. 49).

12. Adam Ulam, *The Unfinished Revolution* (New York, Vintage Books, 1964), p. 97.

13. In 1965, 20 companies out of 420,000 made 38% of profits after taxes, and earnings on foreign investments were well over three times what they were 15 years earlier. The sales of GM exceeded the GNP of all but nine foreign countries. The 10 largest companies reported profits equal to the next 490. One thousand companies disappeared through merger.

14. "America in the Technetronic Age," *Encounter,* Vol. 30 (January 1968), pp. 16–26.

15. "Marxian Socialism in the United States," in Donald D. Egbert and S. Persons, eds., *Socialism and American Life* (Princeton, N.J., Princeton University Press, 1952), Vol. 1, p. 329.

16. *Op. cit.,* p. 5. Less typical, and more realistic, is his belief that these problems also "seem to defy the social scientist's expertise." For some general discussions of this "generosity," see, for example, David Horowitz, *Hemispheres North and South* (Baltimore, The Johns Hopkins Press, 1966), and many special studies. American public officials do not share this faith in our generosity, by and

large. For example, the Assistant Secretary of State for Latin American affairs observed bluntly that "the State Department is not disposed to favor large loans of public funds to countries not welcoming our private capital" (*State Department Bulletin* No. 22, 1950, cited in Frederick Clairmonte, *Economic Liberalism and Underdevelopment* [Bombay and London, Asia Publishing House, 1960], p. 248). Eugene Black, testifying before Congress on the Asian Development Bank, pointed out that "when the Bank makes loans you have international bids, and I am sure that with our ability and ingenuity in this country, we will get our share of the business. We certainly ought to get more than the small amount we contribute." David Bell testified that "the Bank will play a major role in carrying forward another policy of our own assistance program—strengthening the role of the private sector . . . by identifying particular projects which can attract private capital, by helping to draw up development plans and stimulate policies which will encourage private initiative, and by drawing private capital to the region." Nothing here about "the generosity that characterizes our policy."

Equally revealing is the history of programs such as the Alliance for Progress. As Senator Gore commented, this program "has in large measure come to be a subsidy for American business and American exporters" (*Congressional Record,* July 22, 1966)—a fairly accurate judgment, so it appears. For example, the AID lending program in Latin America, according to former Alliance for Progress official William Rogers (*The Twilight Struggle* [New York, Random House, 1967], p. 205), is based on two elements: "a demonstrated balance of payments needed to increase the nation's ability to import U.S. goods and services, and the adoption of public policies and programs which would insure against capital flight on the international account side or the misuse of domestic resources through inefficient budgeting, reduced local savings or inflation." Commenting on this, Robert Smith notes that "the latter standard included increased tax revenues, reduction of budget deficit, elimination of 'distorting subsidies to public activities,' and the adoption of 'state incentives to private sector investment and growth.' " (*New Politics,* Vol. 6 [Spring 1967], pp. 49–57. For some remarks on the other side of our assistance program, military aid, see the articles by James Petras in this and the preceding issue.)

17. "To Intervene or Not to Intervene," *Foreign Affairs,* Vol. 45 (April 1967), pp. 425–36.

18. *New York Times,* December 20, 1967. The *Times* refers to what is printed as "excerpts," but it is not materially different from the full document. I understand that it has since been signed by many other scholars.

19. See the reviews by Coral Bell and B. R. O'G. Anderson in the *China Quarterly,* No. 28 (October-December 1966), pp. 140–43. It should be noted that opposition to social change, and support for the counterrevolutionary violence that is used to suppress it, are longstanding features of American cultural history. Thus according to American historian Louis Hartz, "there is no doubt that the appearance of even a mild socialism in 1848, of Ledru Rollin and the national workshops, was enough to produce general American dismay. There was no outcry in America against the suppression of the June revolt of the workers in Paris, as there was none over the suppression of the Communards in 1871. Here was violence, and plenty of it, but it was being used for order and law, as one editorial writer put it [in the *New York Journal of Commerce*]." (*The Nature of Revolution,* Testimony before the Senate Committee on Foreign Relations, February 26, 1968 [Washington, Government Printing Office, 1968].)

20. "The Public and the Polity," in Ithiel de Sola Pool, ed., *Contemporary Political Science: Toward Empirical Theory* (New York, McGraw-Hill Book Company, 1967), p. 26.

21. Clairmonte, *op. cit.,* p. 325.

22. Recent confirmatory evidence is given by George M. Kahin, in a memorandum of April 13, 1967, in the *Congressional Record.* He cites the Marine Corps estimate that in this province, the principal area of marine strength, 18 out of 549 hamlets had been "secured."

23. Albert Shaw, editor of the *American Review of Reviews,* commenting, in 1893, on America's failure to acquire colonies. Cited in Ernest R. May, *Imperial Democracy* (New York, Harcourt, Brace & World, Inc., 1961), p. 23.

24. Quoted by Robert Guillain in *Le Monde,* May 25, 1966; reprinted, in English translation, as *Vietnam, the Dirty War* (London, Housmans, 1966).

25. According to Jonathan Randal (*New York Times,* June 11, 1967), "only one officer above the rank of lieutenant colonel did not serve in the French army against the Vietminh in the French Indochina war."

26. Douglas Pike, *Viet Cong* (Cambridge, Mass., The M.I.T. Press, 1966), pp. 361–62.

27. *Vietnam: A Dragon Embattled* (New York, Frederick A. Praeger, Inc., 1967), Vol. 2, p. 952. See also note 29.

28. *World Communism* (1939; reprinted Ann Arbor, University of Michigan, 1962), p. 24.

29. *Op. cit.,* Vol. 2, p. 856. As Buttinger explains, "Local elections would have given the Vietminh control of most of the rural communities. The Vietminh was not only popular and in effective political control of large regions, but it alone had people with the requisite organizational skills to exploit whatever opportunities for democratic self-expression the regime opened up." He adds that "the NLF was truly the Vietminh reborn," and speaks of "the similarity, or better, near identity, of the Vietminh and the NLF."

30. Roger Hilsman, "Internal War: The New Communist Tactic," in Franklin Mark Osanka, ed., *Modern Guerrilla Warfare* (New York, The Free Press, 1962), p. 460.

31. Alastair Buchan, director of the Institute for Strategic Studies in London, describes the South Koreans as an "organization of Asian 'black and tans' " ("Questions about Vietnam," *Encounter,* Vol. 30 [January 1968], pp. 3–12).

On the reasons for the remarkable success of pacification in Binh Dinh Province, see Bernard Fall, *Last Reflections on a War* (Garden City, N.Y., Doubleday & Company, Inc., 1967), p. 159. This was one of "the areas where American-Korean multidivision operations have literally smothered the opposition" with "vast search-and-destroy operations" and continuing "tight military control"—or so it seemed, until late 1967, and finally February 1968, when the lid blew off. A report on Binh Dinh Province, the "showcase" province for pacification, in the *New York Times,* February 20, tells the story. "The enemy moves in December—which several military men called a 'softening up' for the offensive—resulted in a wave of allied air strikes on villages. Hundreds of homes were destroyed"—the standard American response. An American official reports: "What the Vietcong did was occupy the hamlets we pacified just for the purpose of having the allies move in and bomb them out. By their presence, the hamlets were destroyed." No doubt our psychological warfare specialists are now explaining to the Vietnamese, who seem to have some difficulty understanding these subtleties, that the destruction of the villages is the fault of the Vietcong. In any event, the report continues, "the entire 1968 program for the province has now been shelved" and "the program is now set back anywhere from 14 to 18 months"—that is, back to the time of the initial saturation with American and Korean troops. "It has all gone down the drain," said one gloomy American official.

32. *United States Policy and the Third World* (Boston, Little, Brown and Company, 1967), Ch. 3.

33. Morton H. Halperin, *Contemporary Military Strategy* (Boston, Little, Brown and Company, 1967), pp. 141–2. I am indebted to Herbert P. Bix for bringing this contribution to the social sciences to my attention.

34. Wolf, *op. cit.,* p. 69.

35. There is little point in a lengthy discussion of Wolf's concept of international affairs or his empirical studies. To take a few examples, he assumes without question that North Vietnam's willingness to "disrupt the regime" in the South was motivated in part by "the marked economic and social improvements accomplished by the Diem regime from 1955 to 1960—dramatic by comparison with the economic stagnation in North Vietnam" (for fact rather than fancy on relative development, see Buttinger, *op. cit.,* Vol. 2, pp. 928, 966 f.); and also that India's "moderately successful growth" was part of the motivation behind "China's aggressive actions in October 1962." See also note 36. As to the solidity of Wolf's empirical studies, it is perhaps enough to note that his most significant result, the correlation between higher GNP and higher level of political democracy in Latin America, arises principally from the conclusion (based on data from 1950 to 1960) that Brazil and Argentina (along with Mexico and Chile) rank high on the scale of political democracy (cf. p. 124). The general level of sophistication is illustrated, for example, by a solemn reference to a consultant for having explained that in determining the "total military value" of a set of alternatives, it is not enough to sum up the separate values; one must also weight responses by probability of occurrence.

36. "But in all cases, the primary consideration should be whether the proposed measure is likely to increase the cost and difficulties of insurgent operations and help to disrupt the insurgent organization, rather than whether it wins popular loyalty and support, or whether it contributes to a more productive, efficient, or equitable use of resources" (Wolf, *op. cit.,* p. 69). We must understand that "successful counterinsurgency programs can be conducted among a rural populace that is passive or even hostile, rather than loyal, to the government." As evidence, Wolf cites his belief that "The growth of the Viet Cong and of the Pathet Lao probably occurred despite the opposition of a

large majority of the people in both Vietnam and Laos" (*ibid.*, p. 48). If they can do it, so can we.

In contrast, Robert Scigliano (of the Michigan State University Vietnam Advisory Group) reported that "using the estimate of American officials in Saigon at the end of 1962, about one-half of the South Vietnamese support the NLF" (*South Vietnam: Nation Under Stress* [Boston, Houghton Mifflin Company, 1963], p. 145). Arthur Dommen reports (*Conflict in Laos: The Politics of Neutralization* [New York, Frederick A. Praeger, Inc., 1964]) that "the Pathet Lao needed no propaganda to turn the rural population against the townspeople" (p. 107). The American Mission took care of this, with its lavish aid (1/2 of 1 percent of which was spent on agriculture, the livelihood of 96 percent of the population) leading to immense corruption, the proliferation of luxurious villas and large automobiles alongside of grinding poverty; and with its constant subversion in support, first of the "pro-Western neutralist" Phoui Sananikone, and then of the military dictator Phoumi Nosavan. As Roger Hilsman puts it, the real Pathet Lao "threat" was "expansion of political control based on winning peasant support in the villages" (*To Move a Nation* [Garden City, N.Y., Doubleday & Company, Inc., 1967], p. 112). The lack of support for the Pathet Lao was amply demonstrated in the 1958 elections, in which 9 of their 13 candidates won, and Souphanouvong, the leading Pathet Lao figure, received more votes than any other candidate in the country. It was this election victory that set off the American attempts at subversion. As Dommen says, "once again the United States threw its support to the most feudal elements of the society."

To Charles Wolf, all of this demonstrates that counterinsurgency, like insurgency, can succeed without concern for popular loyalty and participation.

37. Cited in Clairmonte, *op. cit.*, p. 92. The ancestors of whom Merivale speaks are those who crushed the Indian textile industry by embargoes and import duties, as was quite necessary. "Had this not been the case, the mills of Paisley and Manchester would have been stopped in their outset, and could scarcely have been again set in motion, even by the power of steam. They were created by the sacrifice of Indian manufacturers" (Horace Wilson, 1826, cited by Clairmonte, p. 87).

This is the classic example of the creation of underdevelopment through imperialism. For a detailed study of this process see André Gunder Frank,

Capitalism and Underdevelopment in Latin America (New York, Monthly Review Press, 1967).

38. See Robert E. Osgood, *Ideals and Self-Interest in America's Foreign Relations* (Chicago, University of Chicago Press, 1953), pp. 72–73.

39. "Some Reflections on U.S. Policy in Southeast Asia," in William Henderson, ed., *Southeast Asia: Problems of United States Policy* (Cambridge, Mass., The M.I.T. Press, 1963), pp. 249–63. This collection of papers was published with the encouragement of the Asia Society because of "the scholarly quality of the papers and their enlightening contribution to the formation of United States policy in the area."

40. *Thailand and the United States* (Washington, Public Affairs Press, 1965).

41. The Bank of America placed a full-page ad in the Fourth of July edition, 1951, of the *Bangkok Post* saluting the kingdom of Thailand with these words: "In both Thailand and America democracy has gone hand in hand with national sovereignty. Today both nations stand in the forefront of world efforts to promote and defend the democratic way of life."

42. In an article on "U.S.-Thai links" in the *Christian Science Monitor*, October 14, 1967.

43. Just a few paragraphs earlier we read that in the postwar period "the Americans rapidly expanded the Thai armed forces from 50,000 to 100,000 men . . . the United States quickly increased the police forces, and this helped suppress opponents of the government. The technical assistance program was largely converted to military objectives. The internal impact of this policy further strengthened the power and prestige of the Thai military leaders who had seized the government in 1947. The effort to move toward some form of constitutional rule was halted, and the democratic institutions inaugurated by civilian leaders just after the war were abolished. Political parties were suppressed. The press was censored. Power became increasingly centralized in the hands of a few military leaders." All of this, however, did not constitute "interference in the domestic affairs of other nations," and is not "contrary to American traditions."

44. *Western Interests in the Pacific Realm* (New York, Random House, 1967).

45. Of what importance, then, is the fact that the overwhelming majority of Okinawans, including 80% of those whose businesses would be impaired or destroyed by this move, want the island returned to Japan, according to the *Asahi* polls (see *Japan Quarterly*, Vol. 15 [January–March 1968], pp. 42–52)? As to the "strategic trust territories," Adam says, we must also not become overly senti-

mental: "A strategic trust is based on the assumption of the overriding importance of national defense and the preservation of world order as against the
cultural and political freedom of the indigenous inhabitants."

46. H. D. Malaviya, quoted in Clairmonte (*op. cit.,* p. 114), who cites substantial
evidence in support of the following evaluation of the consequences of Western dominance: "The systematic destruction of Indian manufacturers; the
creation of the Zemindari [landed aristocracy] and its parasitical outgrowths;
the changes in agrarian structure; the financial losses incurred by tribute; the
sharp transition from a premonetised economy to one governed by the international price mechanism—these were some of the social and institutional
forces that were to bring the apocalypse of death and famine to millions—
with few or no compensatory benefits to the ryot [peasant]" (p. 107). See also
note 37.

47. Cited in Paul Avrich, *The Russian Anarchists* (Princeton, N.J., Princeton University Press, 1967), pp. 93–94. A recent reformulation of this view is given by
Anton Pannekoek, the Dutch scientist and spokesman for libertarian communism, in his *Workers Councils* (Melbourne, 1950), pp. 36–37:

It is not for the first time that a ruling class tries to explain, and so to per-
petuate, its rule as the consequences of an inborn difference between two
kinds of people, one destined by nature to ride, the other to be ridden.
The landowning aristocracy of former centuries defended their privileged position by boasting their extraction from a nobler race of con-
querors that had subdued the lower race of common people. Big capitalists
explain their dominating place by the assertion that they have brains and
other people have none. In the same way now especially the intellectuals,
considering themselves the rightful rulers of to-morrow, claim their spiritual superiority. They form the rapidly increasing class of university-
trained officials and free professions, specialized in mental work, in study
of books and of science, and they consider themselves as the people most
gifted with intellect. Hence they are destined to be leaders of the production, whereas the ungifted mass shall execute the manual work, for which
no brains are needed. They are no defenders of capitalism; not capital, but
intellect should direct labor. The more so, since now society is such a
complicated structure, based on abstract and difficult science, that only the
highest intellectual acumen is capable of embracing, grasping and han-
dling it. Should the working masses, from lack of insight, fail to acknowl-

edge this need of superior intellectual lead, should they stupidly try to take the direction into their own hands, chaos and ruin will be the inevitable consequence.

48. See note 7. Albert Parry has suggested that there are important similarities between the emergence of a scientific elite in the Soviet Union and the United States, in their growing role in decision making, citing Bell's thesis in support. See the *New York Times*, March 27, 1966, reporting on the Midwest Slavic Conference.

49. Letter to Herzen and Ogareff, 1866, cited in Daniel Guérin, *Jeunesse du socialisme libertoire* (Paris, Librairie Marcel Rivière, 1959), p. 119.

50. Rosa Luxemburg, *The Russian Revolution,* trans. Bertram D. Wolfe (Ann Arbor, University of Michigan Press, 1961), p. 71.

51. Luxemburg, cited by Guérin, *Jeunesse du socialisme libertaire,* pp. 106–7.

52. *Leninism or Marxism,* in Luxemburg, *op. cit.,* p. 102.

53. For a very enlightening study of this matter, emphasizing domestic issues, see Michael Paul Rogin, *The Intellectuals and McCarthy: The Radical Specter* (Cambridge, Mass., the M.I.T. Press, 1967).

54. *The Spanish Republic and the Civil War: 1931–1939* (Princeton, N.J., Princeton University Press, 1965).

55. Respectively, President of the Republic, Prime Minister from May until the Franco insurrection, and member of the conservative wing of the Popular Front selected by Azaña to try to set up a compromise government after the insurrection.

56. It is interesting that Douglas Pike's very hostile account of the National Liberation Front, cited earlier, emphasizes the popular and voluntary element in its striking organizational successes. What he describes, whether accurately or not one cannot tell, is a structure of interlocking self-help organizations, loosely coordinated and developed through persuasion rather than force—in certain respects, of a character that would have appealed to anarchist thinkers. Those who speak so freely of the "authoritarian Vietcong" may be correct, but they have presented little evidence to support their judgment. Of course, it must be understood that Pike regards the element of voluntary mass participation in self-help associations as the most dangerous and insidious feature of the NLF organizational structure.

Also relevant is the history of collectivization in China, which, as compared with the Soviet Union, shows a much higher reliance on persuasion and mutual aid than on force and terror, and appears to have been more successful. See Thomas P. Bernstein, "Leadership and Mass Mobilisation in the Soviet and Chinese Collectivization Campaigns of 1929–30 and 1955–56: A Comparison," *China Quarterly,* No. 31 (July–September 1967), pp. 1–47, for some interesting and suggestive comments and analysis.

The scale of the Chinese Revolution is so great and reports in depth are so fragmentary that it would no doubt be foolhardy to attempt a general evaluation. Still, all the reports I have been able to study suggest that insofar as real successes were achieved in the several stages of land reform, mutual aid, collectivization, and formation of communes, they were traceable in large part to the complex interaction of the Communist party cadres and the gradually evolving peasant associations, a relation which seems to stray far from the Leninist model of organization. This is particularly evident in William Hinton's magnificent study *Fanshen* (New York, Monthly Review Press, 1966), which is unparalleled, to my knowledge, as an analysis of a moment of profound revolutionary change. What seems to me particularly striking in his account of the early stages of revolution in one Chinese village is not only the extent to which party cadres submitted themselves to popular control, but also, and more significant, the ways in which exercise of control over steps of the revolutionary process was a factor in developing the consciousness and insight of those who took part in the revolution, not only from a political and social point of view, but also with respect to the human relationships that were created. It is interesting, in this connection, to note the strong populist element in early Chinese Marxism. For some very illuminating observations about this general matter, see Maurice Meisner, *Li Ta-chao and the Origins of Chinese Marxism* (Cambridge, Mass., Harvard University Press, 1967).

I am not suggesting that the anarchist revolution in Spain—with its background of more than thirty years of education and struggle—is being relived in Asia, but rather that the spontaneous and voluntary elements in popular mass movements have probably been seriously misunderstood because of the instinctive antipathy towards such phenomena among intellectuals, and more recently, because of the insistence on interpreting them in terms of Cold War mythology.

57. "The Spanish Background," *New Left Review,* No. 40 (November–December 1966), pp. 85–90.

58. José Peirats, *La C.N.T. en la revolución española* (Toulouse, Ediciones C.N.T., 1951–52), 3 vols. Jackson makes one passing reference to it. Peirats has since

published a general history of the period, *Los anarquistas en la crisis politica española* (Buenos Aires, Editorial Alfa-Argentina, 1964). This highly informative book should certainly be made available to an English-speaking audience.

59. An exception to the rather general failure to deal with the anarchist revolution is Hugh Thomas' "Anarchist Agrarian Collectives in the Spanish Civil War," in Martin Gilbert, ed., *A Century of Conflict, 1850–1950: Essays for A. J. P. Taylor* (New York, Atheneum Publishers, 1967), pp. 245–63. See note 106 below for some discussion. There is also much useful information in what to my mind is the best general history of the Civil War, *La Révolution et la guerre d'Espagne,* by Pierre Broué and Émile Témime (Paris, Les Éditions de Minuit, 1961). A concise and informative recent account is contained in Daniel Guérin, *L'Anarchisme* (Paris, Gallimard, 1965). In his extensive study, *The Spanish Civil War* (New York, Harper & Row, Publishers, 1961; paperback ed. 1963), Hugh Thomas barely refers to the popular revolution, and some of the major events are not mentioned at all—see, for example, note 97 below.

60. *Collectivisations: l'oeuvre constructive de la Révolution espagnole,* 2nd ed. (Toulouse, Éditions C.N.T., 1965). The first edition was published in Barcelona (Éditions C.N.T.-F.A.I., 1937). There is an excellent and sympathetic summary by the Marxist scholar Karl Korsch, "Collectivization in Spain," in *Living Marxism,* Vol. 4 (April 1939), pp. 179–82. In the same issue (pp. 170–71), the liberal-Communist reaction to the Spanish Civil War is summarized succinctly, and I believe accurately, as follows: "With their empty chatter as to the wonders of Bolshevik discipline, the geniality of Caballero, and the passions of the Pasionaria, the 'modern liberals' merely covered up their real desire for the destruction of all revolutionary possibilities in the Civil War, and their preparation for the possible war over the Spanish issue in the interest of their diverse fatherlands . . . what was truly revolutionary in the Spanish Civil War resulted from the direct actions of the workers and pauperized peasants, and not because of a specific form of labor organization nor an especially gifted leadership." I think that the record bears out this analysis, and I also think that it is this fact that accounts for the distaste for the revolutionary phase of the Civil War and its neglect in historical scholarship.

61. An illuminating eyewitness account of this period is that of Franz Borkenau, *The Spanish Cockpit* (1938; reprinted Ann Arbor, University of Michigan Press, 1963).

62. Figures from Guérin, *L'Anarchisme,* p. 154.

63. A useful account of this period is given by Felix Morrow, *Revolution and Counter-Revolution in Spain* (1938; reprinted London, New Park Publications, 1963).

64. Cited by Camillo Berneri in his "Lettre ouverte à la camarade Frederica [sic] Montseny," *Guerre de classes en Espagne* (Paris, 1946), a collection of items translated from his journal *Guerra di Classe.* Berneri was the outstanding anarchist intellectual in Spain. He opposed the policy of joining the government and argued for an alternative, more typically anarchist strategy to which I will return below. His own view towards joining the government was stated succinctly by a Catalan worker whom he quotes, with reference to the Republic of 1931: "It is always the old dog with a new collar." Events were to prove the accuracy of this analysis.

Berneri had been a leading spokesman of Italian anarchism. He left Italy after Mussolini's rise to power, and came to Barcelona on July 19, 1936. He formed the first Italian units for the antifascist war, according to anarchist historian Rudolf Rocker (*The Tragedy of Spain* [New York, Freie Arbeiter Stimme, 1937], p. 44). He was murdered, along with his older comrade Barbieri, during the May Days of 1937. (Arrested on May 5 by the Communist-controlled police, he was shot during the following night.) Hugh Thomas, in *The Spanish Civil War,* p. 428, suggests that "the assassins may have been Italian Communists" rather than the police. Thomas' book, which is largely devoted to military history, mentions Berneri's murder but makes no other reference to his ideas or role.

Berneri's name does not appear in Jackson's history.

65. Burnett Bolloten, *The Grand Camouflage: The Communist Conspiracy in the Spanish Civil War* (New York, Frederick A. Praeger, Inc., 1961), p. 86. This book, by a UP correspondent in Spain during the Civil War, contains a great deal of important documentary evidence bearing on the questions considered here. The attitude of the wealthy farmers of this area, most of them former supporters of the right-wing organizations that had now disappeared, is well described by the general secretary of the Peasant Federation, Julio Mateu: "Such is the sympathy for us [that is, the Communist party] in the Valencia countryside that hundreds and thousands of farmers would join our party if we were to let them. These farmers . . . love our party like a sacred thing . . . they [say] 'The Communist Party is our party.' Comrades, what emotion the peasants display when they utter these words" (cited in Bolloten, p. 86). There is some interesting speculation about the backgrounds for the

writing of this very important book in H. R. Southworth, *Le mythe de la croisade de Franco* (Ruedo Ibérico, Paris, 1964; Spanish edition, same publisher, 1963).

The Communist headquarters in Valencia had on the wall two posters: "Respect the property of the small peasant" and "Respect the property of the small industrialist" (Borkenau, *The Spanish Cockpit,* p. 117). Actually, it was the rich farmer as well who sought protection from the Communists, whom Borkenau describes as constituting the extreme right wing of the Republican forces. By early 1937, according to Borkenau, the Communist party was "to a large extent . . . the party of the military and administrative personnel, in the second place the party of the petty bourgeoisie and certain well-to-do peasant groups, in the third place the party of the employees, and only in the fourth place the party of the industrial workers" (p. 192). The party also attracted many police and army officers. The police chief in Madrid and the chief of intelligence, for example, were party members. In general, the party, which had been insignificant before the revolution, "gave the urban and rural middle classes a powerful access of life and vigour" as it defended them from the revolutionary forces (Bolloten, *op. cit.,* p. 86). Gerald Brenan describes the situation as follows, in *The Spanish Labyrinth* (1943; reprinted Cambridge, Cambridge University Press, 1960), p. 325:

> Unable to draw to themselves the manual workers, who remained firmly fixed in their unions, the Communists found themselves the refuge for all those who had suffered from the excesses of the Revolution or who feared where it might lead them. Well-to-do Catholic orange-growers in Valencia, peasants in Catalonia, small shopkeepers and business men, Army officers and Government officials enrolled in their ranks. . . . Thus [in Catalonia] one had a strange and novel situation: on the one side stood the huge compact proletariat of Barcelona with its long revolutionary tradition, and on the other the white-collar workers and *petite bourgeoisie* of the city, organized and armed by the Communist party against it.

Actually, the situation that Brenan describes is not as strange a one as he suggests. It is, rather, a natural consequence of Bolshevik elitism that the "Red bureaucracy" should act as a counterrevolutionary force except under the conditions where its present or future representatives are attempting to seize power for themselves, in the name of the masses whom they pretend to represent.

66. Bolloten, *op. cit.*, p. 189. The legalization of revolutionary actions already undertaken and completed recalls the behavior of the "revolutionary vanguard" in the Soviet Union in 1918. Cf. Arthur Rosenberg, *A History of Bolshevism* (1932; republished in translation from the original German, New York, Russell and Russell, Publishers, 1965), Ch. 6. He describes how the expropriations, "accomplished as the result of spontaneous action on the part of workers and against the will of the Bolsheviks," were reluctantly legalized by Lenin months later and then placed under central party control. On the relation of the Bolsheviks to the anarchists in postrevolutionary Russia, interpreted from a pro-anarchist point of view, see Guérin, *L'Anarchisme,* pp. 96–125. See also Avrich, *op. cit.*, Part II, pp. 123–254.

67. Bolloten, *op. cit.*, p. 191.

68. *Ibid.*, p. 194.

69. For some details, see Vernon Richards, *Lessons of the Spanish Revolution* (London, Freedom Press, 1953), pp. 83–88.

70. For a moving eyewitness account, see George Orwell, *Homage to Catalonia* (1938; reprinted New York, Harcourt, Brace & World, 1952, and Boston, Beacon Press, 1955; quotations in this book from Beacon Press edition). This brilliant book received little notice at the time of its first publication, no doubt because the picture Orwell drew was in sharp conflict with established liberal dogma. The attention that it has received as a cold-war document since its republication in 1952 would, I suspect, have been of little comfort to the author.

71. Cited by Rocker, *The Tragedy of Spain,* p. 28.

72. See *ibid.* for a brief review. It was a great annoyance to Hitler that these interests were, to a large extent, protected by Franco.

73. *Ibid.*, p. 35.

74. *Op. cit.*, pp. 324 f.

75. Borkenau, *The Spanish Cockpit,* pp. 289–92. It is because of the essential accuracy of Borkenau's account that I think Hobsbawm (*op. cit.*) is quite mistaken in believing that the Communist policy "was undoubtedly the only one which could have won the Civil War." In fact, the Communist policy was bound to fail, because it was predicated on the assumption that the Western democracies would join the antifascist effort if only Spain could be preserved as, in effect, a Western colony. Once the Communist leaders saw the futility of this hope, they abandoned the struggle, which was not in their eyes an effort to win the Civil War, but only to serve the interests of Russian foreign policy.

I also disagree with Hobsbawm's analysis of the anarchist revolution, cited earlier, for reasons that are implicit in this entire discussion.

76. *Op. cit.,* pp. 143–44.

77. Cited by Rosenberg, *op. cit.,* pp. 168–69.

78. Bolloten, *op. cit.,* p. 84.

79. *Ibid.,* p. 85. As noted earlier, the "small farmer" included the prosperous orange growers, etc. (see note 65).

80. Brenan, *op. cit.,* p. 321.

81. Correspondence from Companys to Prieto, 1939. While Companys, as a Catalonian with separatist impulses, would naturally be inclined to defend Catalonian achievements, he was surely not sympathetic to collectivization, despite his cooperative attitude during the period when the anarchists, with real power in their hands, permitted him to retain nominal authority. I know of no attempt to challenge the accuracy of his assessment. Morrow (*op. cit.,* p. 77) quotes the Catalonian Premier, the entrepreneur Juan Tarradellas, as defending the administration of the collectivized war industries against a Communist (PSUC) attack, which he termed the "most arbitrary falsehoods." There are many other reports commenting on the functioning of the collectivized industries by nonanarchist firsthand observers, that tend to support Companys. For example, the Swiss socialist Andres Oltmares is quoted by Rocker (*The Tragedy of Spain,* p. 24) as saying that after the revolution the Catalonian workers' syndicates "in seven weeks accomplished fully as much as France did in fourteen months after the outbreak of the World War." Continuing, he says:

> In the midst of the civil war the Anarchists have proved themselves to be political organizers of the first rank. They kindled in everyone the required sense of responsibility, and knew how by eloquent appeals to keep alive the spirit of sacrifice for the general welfare of the people.
>
> As a Social Democrat I speak here with inner joy and sincere admiration of my experience in Catalonia. The anti-capitalist transformation took place here without their having to resort to a dictatorship. The members of the syndicates are their own masters, and carry on production and the distribution of the products of labor under their own management with the advice of technical experts in whom they have confidence. The enthusiasm of the workers is so great that they scorn any personal advantage and are concerned only for the welfare of all.

Even Borkenau concludes, rather grudgingly, that industry was functioning fairly well, as far as he could see. The matter deserves a serious study.

82. Quoted in Richards, *op. cit.,* pp. 46–47.

83. *Ibid.* Richards suggests that the refusal of the central government to support the Aragon front may have been motivated in part by the general policy of counterrevolution. "This front, largely manned by members of the C.N.T.-F.A.I., was considered of great strategic importance by the anarchists, having as its ultimate objective the linking of Catalonia with the Basque country and Asturias, i.e., a linking of the industrial region [of Catalonia] with an important source of raw materials." Again, it would be interesting to undertake a detailed investigation of this topic.

That the Communists withheld arms from the Aragon front seems established beyond question, and it can hardly be doubted that the motivation was political. See, for example, D. T. Cattell, *Communism and the Spanish Civil War* (1955; reprinted New York, Russell and Russell, Publishers, 1965), p. 110. Cattell, who in general bends over backwards to try to justify the behavior of the central government, concludes that in this case there is little doubt that the refusal of aid was politically motivated. Brenan takes the same view, claiming that the Communists "kept the Aragon front without arms to spite the Anarchists." The Communists resorted to some of the most grotesque slanders to explain the lack of arms on the Aragon front; for example, the *Daily Worker* attributed the arms shortage to the fact that "the Trotskyist General Kopp had been carting enormous supplies of arms and ammunition across no-man's land to the fascists" (cited by Morrow, *op. cit.,* p. 145). As Morrow points out, George Kopp is a particularly bad choice as a target for such accusations. His record is well known, for example, from the account given by Orwell, who served under his command (see Orwell, *op. cit.,* pp. 209 f.). Orwell was also able to refute, from firsthand observation, many of the other absurdities that were appearing in the liberal press about the Aragon front, for example, the statement by Ralph Bates in the *New Republic* that the POUM troops were "playing football with the Fascists in no man's land." At that moment, as Orwell observes, "the P.O.U.M. troops were suffering heavy casualties and a number of my personal friends were killed and wounded."

84. Cited in *Living Marxism,* p. 172.

85. Bolloten, *op. cit.,* p. 49, comments on the collectivization of the dairy trade in Barcelona, as follows: "The Anarchosyndicalists eliminated as unhygienic over forty pasteurizing plants, pasteurized all the milk in the remaining nine,

and proceeded to displace all dealers by establishing their own dairies. Many of the retailers entered the collective, but some refused to do so: 'They asked for a much higher wage than that paid to the workers . . . , claiming that they could not manage on the one allotted to them' [*Tierra y Libertad*, August 21, 1937—the newspaper of the FAI, the anarchist activists]." His information is primarily from anarchist sources, which he uses much more extensively than any historian other than Peirats. He does not present any evaluation of these sources, which—like all others—must be used critically.

86. Morrow, *op. cit.*, p. 136.
87. Borkenau, *The Spanish Cockpit*, p. 182.
88. *Ibid.*, p. 183.
89. *Ibid.*, p. 184. According to Borkenau, "it is doubtful whether Comorera is personally responsible for this scarcity; it might have arisen anyway, in pace with the consumption of the harvest." This speculation may or may not be correct. Like Borkenau, we can only speculate as to whether the village and workers' committees would have been able to continue to provision Barcelona, with or without central administration, had it not been for the policy of "abstract liberalism," which was of a piece with the general Communist-directed attempts to destroy the Revolutionary organizations and the structures developed in the Revolutionary period.
90. Orwell, *op. cit.*, pp. 109–11. Orwell's description of Barcelona in December (pp. 4–5), when he arrived for the first time, deserves more extensive quotation:

> It was the first time that I had ever been in a town where the working class was in the saddle. Practically every building of any size had been seized by the workers and was draped with red flags or with the red and black flag of the Anarchists; every wall was scrawled with the hammer and sickle and with the initials of the revolutionary parties; almost every church had been gutted and its images burnt. Churches here and there were being systematically demolished by gangs of workmen. Every shop and café had an inscription saying that it had been collectivized; even the bootblacks had been collectivized and their boxes painted red and black. Walters and shop-walkers looked you in the face and treated you as an equal. Servile and even ceremonial forms of speech bad temporarily disappeared. Nobody said "Señor" or "Don" or even "Usted"; everyone called everyone else "Comrade" and "Thou," and said "Salud!" instead of "Buenos dias."

Tipping had been forbidden by law since the time of Primo de Rivera; almost my first experience was receiving a lecture from an hotel manager for trying to tip a lift-boy. There were no private motor cars, they had all been commandeered, and all the trams and taxis and much of the other transport were painted red and black. The revolutionary posters were everywhere, flaming from the walls in clean reds and blues that made the few remaining advertisements look like daubs of mud. Down the Ramblas, the wide central artery of the town where crowds of people streamed constantly to and fro, the loud-speakers were bellowing revolutionary songs all day and far into the night. And it was the aspect of the crowds that was the queerest thing of all. In outward appearance it was a town in which the wealthy classes had practically ceased to exist. Except for a small number of women and foreigners there were no "well-dressed" people at all. Practically everyone wore rough working-class clothes, or blue overalls or some variant of the militia uniform. All this was queer and moving. There was much in it that I did not understand, in some ways I did not even like it, but I recognized it immediately as a state of affairs worth fighting for. Also I believed that things were as they appeared, that this was really a workers' State and that the entire bourgeoisie had either fled, been killed, or voluntarily come over to the workers' side; I did not realize that great numbers of well-to-do bourgeois were simply lying low and disguising themselves as proletarians for the time being . . .

. . . waiting for that happy day when Communist power would reintroduce the old state of society and destroy popular involvement in the war.

In December 1936, however, the situation was still as described in the following remarks (p. 6):

Yet so far as one can judge the people were contented and hopeful. There was no unemployment, and the price of living was still extremely low; you saw very few conspicuously destitute people, and no beggars except the gipsies. Above all, there was a belief in the revolution and the future, a feeling of having suddenly emerged into an era of equality and freedom. Human beings were trying to behave as human beings and not as cogs in the capitalist machine. In the barbers' shops were Anarchist notices (the barbers were mostly Anarchists) solemnly explaining that barbers were no longer slaves. In the streets were coloured posters appealing to prostitutes to stop being prostitutes. To anyone from the hard-boiled, sneering civilization of the English-speaking races there was something rather pathetic in the literalness with which these idealistic Spaniards took the hackneyed phrases of revolution. At that time revolutionary ballads of the naïvest kind, all about proletarian brotherhood and the wickedness of Mussolini, were being sold on the streets for a few centimes each. I have often seen an illiterate militiaman buy one of these ballads, laboriously spell out the words, and then, when he had got the hang of it, begin singing it to an appropriate tune.

Recall the dates. Orwell arrived in Barcelona in late December 1936. Comorera's decree abolishing the workers' supply committees and the bread committees was on January 7. Borkenau returned to Barcelona in mid-January; Orwell, in April.

91. See Bolloten, *op. cit.,* p. 74, citing the anarchist spokesman Juan Peiró, in September 1936. Like other anarchists and left-wing Socialists, Peiró sharply condemns the use of force to introduce collectivization, taking the position that was expressed by most anarchists, as well as by left-wing socialists such as Ricardo Zabalza, general secretary of the Federation of Land Workers, who stated, on January 8, 1937: "I prefer a small, enthusiastic collective, formed by a group of active and honest workers, to a large collective set up by force and composed of peasants without enthusiasm, who would sabotage it until it failed. Voluntary collectivization may seem the longer course, but the example of the small, well-managed collective will attract the entire peasantry, who are profoundly realistic and practical, whereas forced collectivization would end by discrediting socialized agriculture" (cited by Bolloten *op. cit.,* p. 59). However, there seems no doubt that the precepts of the anarchist and left-socialist spokesmen were often violated in practice.

92. Borkenau, *The Spanish Cockpit,* pp. 219–20. Of this officer, Jackson says only that he was "a dependable professional officer." After the fall of Málaga, Lieutenant Colonel Villalba was tried for treason, for having deserted the headquarters and abandoned his troops. Broué and Témime remark that it is difficult to determine what justice there was in the charge.

93. Jesús Hernández and Juan Comorera, *Spain Organises for Victory: The Policy of the Communist Party of Spain Explained* (London, Communist Party of Great Britain, n.d.), cited by Richards, *op. cit.,* pp. 99–100. There was no accusation that the phone service was restricted, but only that the revolutionary workers could maintain "a close check on the conversations that took place between

the politicians." As Richards further observes, "It is, of course, a quite different matter when the 'indiscreet ear' is that of the O.G.P.U."

94. Broué and Témime, *op. cit.,* p. 266.

95. Jackson, *op. cit.,* p. 370. Thomas suggests that Sesé was probably killed accidentally (*The Spanish Civil War,* p. 428).

96. The anarchist mayor of the border town of Puigcerdá had been assassinated in April, after Negrín's carabineros had taken over the border posts. That same day a prominent UGT member, Roldán Cortada, was murdered in Barcelona, it is presumed by CNT militants. This presumption is disputed by Peirats (*Los Anarquistos:* see note 58), who argues, with some evidence, that the murder may have been a Stalinist provocation. In reprisal, a CNT man was killed. Orwell, whose eyewitness account of the May Days is unforgettable, points out that "One can gauge the attitude of the foreign capitalist Press towards the Communist-Anarchist feud by the fact that Roldán's murder was given wide publicity, while the answering murder was carefully unmentioned" (*op. cit.,* p. 119). Similarly, one can gauge Jackson's attitude towards this struggle by his citation of Sesé's murder as a critical event, while the murder of Berneri goes unmentioned (cf. notes 64 and 95). Orwell remarks elsewhere that "In the English press, in particular, you would have to search for a long time before finding any favourable reference, at any period of the war, to the Spanish Anarchists. They have been systematically denigrated, and, as I know by my own experience, it is almost impossible to get anyone to print anything in their defence" (p. 159). Little has changed since.

97. According to Orwell (*op. cit.,* pp. 153–54), "A British cruiser and two British destroyers had closed in upon the harbour, and no doubt there were other warships not far away. The English newspapers gave it out that these ships were proceeding to Barcelona 'to protect British interests,' but in fact they made no move to do so; that is, they did not land any men or take off any refugees. There can be no certainty about this, but it was at least inherently likely that the British Government, which had not raised a finger to save the Spanish Government from Franco, would intervene quickly enough to save it from its own working class." This assumption may well have influenced the leftwing leadership to restrain the Barcelona workers from simply taking control of the whole city, as apparently they could easily have done in the initial stages of the May Days.

Hugh Thomas comments (*The Spanish Civil War,* p. 428) that there was "no reason" for Orwell's "apprehension" on this matter. In the light of the

British record with regard to Spain, it seems to me that Thomas is simply unrealistic, as compared with Orwell, in this respect.

98. Orwell, *op. cit.,* pp. 143–44.

99. *Controversy,* August 1937, cited by Morrow, p. 173. The prediction was incor-
rect, though not unreasonable. Had the Western powers and the Soviet
Union wished, compromise would have been possible, it appears, and Spain
might have been saved the terrible consequences of a Franco victory. See Brenan, *op. cit.,* p. 331. He attributes the British failure to support an armistice and
possible reconciliation to the fact that Chamberlain "saw nothing disturbing
in the prospect of an Italian and German victory." It would be interesting to
explore more fully the attitude of Winston Churchill. In April 1937 he stated
that a Franco victory would not harm British interests. Rather, the danger
was a "success of the trotskyists and anarchists" (cited by Broué and Témime,
op. cit., p. 172). Of some interest, in this connection, is the recent discovery of
an unpublished Churchill essay written in March 1939—six months after
Munich—in which he said that England "would welcome and aid a genuine
Hitler of peace and toleration" (see *New York Times,* December 12, 1965).

100. I find no mention at all in Hugh Thomas, *The Spanish Civil War.* The account
here is largely taken from Broué and Témime, pp. 279–80.

101. *Op cit.,* p. 405. A footnote comments on the "leniency" of the government to
those arrested. Jackson has nothing to say about the charges against Ascaso
and others, or the manner in which the old order was restored in Aragon.

To appreciate these events more fully, one should consider, by comparison, the concern for civil liberties shown by Negrín on the second, antifascist
front. In an interview after the war he explained to John Whitaker (*We Cannot Escape History* [New York, The Macmillan Company, 1943], pp. 116–18)
why his government had been so ineffective in coping with the fifth column,
even in the case of known fascist agents. Negrín explained that "we couldn't
arrest a man on suspicion; we couldn't break with the rules of evidence.
You can't risk arresting an innocent man because you are positive in your
own mind that he is guilty. You prosecute a war, yes; but you also live with
your conscience." Evidently, these scruples did not pertain when it was the
rights of anarchist and socialist workers, rather than fascist agents, that were at
stake.

102. Cf. Broué and Témime, p. 262. Ironically, the government forces included
some anarchist troops, the only ones to enter Barcelona.

103. See Bolloten, *op. cit.,* p. 55, n. 1, for an extensive list of sources.

104. Broué and Témime cite the socialists Alardo Prats, Fenner Brockway, and Carlo Rosselli. Borkenau, on the other hand, suspected that the role of terror was great in collectivization. He cites very little to substantiate his feeling, though some evidence is available from anarchist sources. See note 91 above. Some general remarks on collectivization by Rosselli and Brockway are cited by Rudolf Rocker in his essay "Anarchism and Anarchosyndicalism," n. 1, in Paul Eltzbacher, ed., *Anarchism* (London, Freedom Press, 1960), p. 266:

> Rosselli: In three months Catalonia has been able to set up a new social order on the ruins of an ancient system. This is chiefly due to the Anarchists, who have revealed a quite remarkable sense of proportion, realistic understanding, and organizing ability. . . . All the revolutionary forces of Catalonia have united in a program of Syndicalist-Socialist character . . . Anarcho-Syndicalism, hitherto so despised, has revealed itself as a great constructive force. I am no Anarchist, but I regard it as my duty to express here my opinion of the Anarchists of Catalonia, who have all too often been represented as a destructive if not a criminal element.
>
> Brockway: I was impressed by the strength of the C.N.T. It was unnecessary to tell me that it is the largest and most vital of the working class organizations in Spain. That was evident on all sides. The large industries were clearly in the main in the hands of the C.N.T.—railways, road transport, shipping, engineering, textiles, electricity, building, agriculture. . . . I was immensely impressed by the constructive revolutionary work which is being done by the C.N.T. Their achievements of workers' control in industry is an inspiration. . . . There are still some Britishers and Americans who regard the Anarchists of Spain as impossible, undisciplined uncontrollables. This is poles away from the truth. The Anarchists of Spain, through the C.N.T., are doing one of the biggest constructive jobs ever done by the working class. At the front they are fighting Fascism. Behind the front they are actually constructing the new workers' society. They see that the war against Fascism and the carrying through of the social revolution are inseparable. Those who have seen them and understood what they are doing must honor them and be grateful to them. . . . That is surely the biggest thing which has hitherto been done by the workers in any part of the world.

105. Cited by Richards, *op. cit.*, pp. 76–81, where long descriptive quotations are given.

106. See Hugh Thomas, "Anarchist Agrarian Collectives in the Spanish Civil
     War" (note 59). He cites figures showing that agricultural production went up
     in Aragon and Castile, where collectivization was extensive, and down in
     Catalonia and the Levant, where peasant proprietors were the dominant ele-
     ment.

     Thomas' is, to my knowledge, the only attempt by a professional historian
     to assess the data on agricultural collectivization in Spain in a systematic way.
     He concludes that the collectives were probably "a considerable social suc-
     cess" and must have had strong popular support, but he is more doubtful
     about their economic viability. His suggestion that "Communist pressure on
     the collectives may have given them the necessary urge to survive" seems
     quite unwarranted, as does his suggestion that "the very existence of the war
     . . . may have been responsible for some of the success the collectives had."
     On the contrary, their success and spontaneous creation throughout Repub-
     lican Spain suggest that they answered to deeply felt popular sentiments, and
     both the war and Communist pressure appear to have been highly disruptive
     factors—ultimately, of course, destructive factors.

     Other dubious conclusions are that "in respect of redistribution of wealth,
     anarchist collectives were hardly much improvement over capitalism" since
     "no effective way of limiting consumption in richer collectives was devised to
     help poorer ones," and that there was no possibility of developing large-scale
     planning. On the contrary, Bolloten (*op. cit.*, pp. 176–79) points out that "In
     order to remedy the defects of collectivization, as well as to iron out discrep-
     ancies in the living standards of the workers in flourishing and impoverished
     enterprises, the Anarchosyndicalists, although rootedly opposed to national-
     ization, advocated the centralization—or, socialization, as they called it—
     under trade union control, of entire branches of production." He mentions a
     number of examples of partial socialization that had some success, citing as
     the major difficulty that prevented still greater progress the insistence of the
     Communist party and the UGT leadership—though apparently not all of the
     rank-and-file members of the UGT—on government ownership and con-
     trol. According to Richards (*op. cit.*, p. 82): "In June, 1937 . . . a National
     Plenum of Regional Federations of Peasants was held in Valencia to discuss
     the formation of a National Federation of Peasants for the co-ordination and
     extension of the collectivist movement and also to ensure an equitable distri-
     bution of the produce of the land, not only between the collectives but for the
     whole country. Again in Castille in October 1937, a merging of the 100,000

members of the Regional Federation of Peasants and the 13,000 members in the food distributive trades took place. It represented a logical step in ensuring better co-ordination, and was accepted for the whole of Spain at the National Congress of Collectives held in Valencia in November 1937." Still other plans were under consideration for regional and national coordination—see, for example, D. A. de Santillan, *After the Revolution* (New York, Greenberg Publisher, Inc., 1937), for some ideas.

Thomas feels that collectives could not have survived more than "a few years while primitive misery was being overcome." I see nothing in his data to support this conclusion. The Palestinian experience has shown that collectives can remain both a social and an economic success over a long period. The success of Spanish collectivization, under war conditions, seems amazing. One can obviously not be certain whether these successes could have been secured and extended had it not been for the combined fascist, Communist, and liberal attack, but I can find no objective basis for the almost universal skepticism. Again, this seems to me merely a matter of irrational prejudice.

107. The following is a brief description by the anarchist writer Gaston Leval, *Né Franco, Né Stalin, le collettività anarchiche spagnole nella lotta contro Franco e la reazione staliniana* (Milan, Istituto Editoriale Italiano, 1952), pp. 303 f.; sections reprinted in *Collectivités anarchistes en Espagne révolutionnaire, Noir et Rouge,* undated.

In the middle of the month of June, the attack began in Aragon on a grand scale and with hitherto unknown methods. The harvest was approaching. Rifles in hand, treasury guards under Communist orders stopped trucks loaded with provisions on the highways and brought them to their offices. A little later, the same guards poured into the collectives and confiscated great quantities of wheat under the authority of the general staff with headquarters in Barbastro. . . . Later open attacks began, under the command of Lister with troops withdrawn from the front at Belchite more than 50 kilometers away, in the month of August. . . . The final result was that 30 percent of the collectives were completely destroyed. In Alcolea, the municipal council that governed the collective was arrested; the people who lived in the Home for the Aged . . . were thrown out on the street. In Mas de las Matas, in Monzon, in Barbastro, on all sides, there were arrests. Plundering took place everywhere. The stores of the cooperatives and their grain supplies were rifled; furnishings were destroyed. The governor of Aragon, who was appointed by the central government after the dissolution of the Council of Aragon—which appears to have been the signal for the armed attack against the collectives—protested. He was told to go to the devil.

On October 22, at the National Congress of Peasants, the delegation of the Regional Committee of Aragon presented a report of which the following is the summary:

"More than 600 organizers of collectives have been arrested. The government has appointed management committees that seized the warehouses and distributed their contents at random. Land, draught animals, and tools were given to individual families or to the fascists who had been spared by the revolution. The harvest was distributed in the same way. The animals raised by the collectives suffered the same fate. A great number of collectivized pig farms, stables, and dairies were destroyed. In certain communes, such as Bordon and Calaceite, even seed was confiscated and the peasants are now unable to work the land."

The estimate that 30% of the collectives were destroyed is consistent with figures reported by Peirats (*Los anarquistas en la crisis política española*, p. 300). He points out that only 200 delegates attended the congress of collectives of Aragon in September 1937 ("held under the shadow of the bayonets of the Eleventh Division" of Lister) as compared with 500 delegates at the congress of the preceding February. Peirats states that an army division of Catalan separatists and another division of the PSUC also occupied parts of Aragon during this operation, while three anarchist divisions remained at the front, under orders from the CNT-FAI leadership. Compare Jackson's explanation of the occupation of Aragon: "The peasants were known to hate the Consejo, *the anarchists had deserted the front during the Barcelona fighting,* and the very existence of the Consejo was a standing challenge to the authority of the central government" (italics mine).

108. Regarding Bolloten's work, Jackson has this to say: "Throughout the present chapter, I have drawn heavily on this carefully documented study of the Communist Party in 1936–37. It is unrivaled in its coverage of the wartime press, of which Bolloten, himself a UP correspondent in Spain, made a large collection" (p. 363 n.).

109. See note 64. A number of citations from Berneri's writings are given by Broué and Témime. Morrow also presents several passages from his journal,

Guerra di Classe. A collection of his works would be a very useful contribution to our understanding of the Spanish Civil War and to the problems of revolutionary war in general.

110. Cattell, *op. cit.,* p. 208. See also the remarks by Borkenau, Brenan, and Bolloten cited earlier. Neither Cattell nor Borkenau regards this decline of fighting spirit as a major factor, however.

111. *Op. cit.,* p. 195, n. 7.

112. To this extent, Trotsky took a similar position. See his *Lesson of Spain* (London, Workers' International Press, 1937).

113. Cited in Richards, *op. cit.,* p. 23.

114. H. E. Kaminski, *Ceux de Barcelone* (Paris, Les Éditions Denoël, 1937), p. 181. This book contains very interesting observations on anarchist Spain by a skeptical though sympathetic eyewitness.

115. May 15, 1937. Cited by Richards, *op. cit.,* p. 106.

116. Cited by Broué and Témime, *op. cit.,* p. 258, n. 34. The conquest of Saragossa was the goal, never realized, of the anarchist militia in Aragon.

117. *Ibid.,* p. 175.

118. *Ibid.,* p. 193.

119. The fact was not lost on foreign journalists. Morrow (*op. cit.,* p. 68) quotes James Minifie in the *New York Herald Tribune,* April 28, 1937: "A reliable police force is being built up quietly but surely. The Valencia government discovered an ideal instrument for this purpose in the Carabineros. These were formerly customs officers and guards, and always had a good reputation for loyalty. It is reported on good authority that 40,000 have been recruited for this force, and that 20,000 have already been armed and equipped. . . . The anarchists have already noticed and complained about the increased strength of this force at a time when we all know there's little enough traffic coming over the frontiers, land or sea. They realize that it will be used against them." Consider what these soldiers, as well as Lister's division or the *asaltos* described by Orwell, might have accomplished on the Aragon front, for example. Consider also the effect on the militiamen, deprived of arms by the central government, of the knowledge that these well-armed, highly trained troops were liquidating the accomplishments of their revolution.

120. Cited in Rocker, *The Tragedy of Spain,* p. 37.

121. For references, see Bolloten, *op. cit.,* p. 192, n. 12.

122. Cited in Rocker, *The Tragedy of Spain,* p. 37.

123. Liston M. Oak, "Balance Sheet of the Spanish Revolution," *Socialist Review,*

Vol. 6 (September 1937), pp. 7–9, 26. This reference was brought to my attention by William B. Watson. A striking example of the distortion introduced by the propaganda efforts of the 1930s is the strange story of the influential film *The Spanish Earth,* filmed in 1937 by Joris Ivens with a text (written afterwards) by Hemingway—a project that was apparently initiated by Dos Passos. A very revealing account of this matter, and of the perception of the Civil War by Hemingway and Dos Passos, is given in W. B. Watson and Barton Whaley, "The Spanish Earth of Dos Passos and Hemingway," unpublished, 1967. The film dealt with the collectivized village of Fuentidueña in Valencia (a village collectivized by the UGT, incidentally). For the libertarian Dos Passos, the revolution was the dominant theme; it was the antifascist war, however, that was to preoccupy Hemingway. The role of Dos Passos was quickly forgotten, because of the fact (as Watson and Whaley point out) that "Dos Passos had become anathema to the Left for his criticisms of communist policies in Spain."

124. As far as the East is concerned, Rocker (*The Tragedy of Spain,* p. 25) claims that "the Russian press, for reasons that are easily understood, never uttered one least little word about the efforts of the Spanish workers and peasants at social reconstruction." I cannot check the accuracy of this claim, but it would hardly be surprising if it were correct.

125. See Patricia A. M. Van der Esch, *Prelude to War: The International Repercussions of the Spanish Civil War (1935–1939)* (The Hague, Martinus Nijhoff, 1951), p. 47, and Brenan, *op. cit.,* p. 329, n. 1. The conservative character of the Basque government was also, apparently, largely a result of French pressure. See Broué and Témime, *op. cit.,* p. 172, no. 8.

126. See Dante A. Puzzo, *Spain and the Great Powers: 1936–1941* (New York, Columbia University Press, 1962), pp. 86 f. This book gives a detailed and very insightful analysis of the international background of the Civil War.

127. Jules Sauerwein, dispatch to the *New York Times* dated July 26. Cited by Puzzo, *op. cit.,* p. 84.

128. Cf., for example, Jackson, *op. cit.,* pp. 248 f.

129. As reported by Herschel V. Johnson of the American embassy in London; cited by Puzzo, *op. cit.,* p. 100.

130. See Broué and Témime, *op. cit.,* pp. 288–89.

131. Cited by Thomas, *The Spanish Civil War,* p. 531, no. 3. Rocker, *The Tragedy of Spain,* p. 14, quotes (without reference) a proposal by Churchill for a five-year

"neutral dictatorship" to "tranquilize" the country, after which they could "perhaps look for a revival of parliamentary institutions."

132. Puzzo, *op. cit.,* p. 116.

133. *Ibid.,* p. 147. Eden is referring, of course, to the Soviet Union. For an analysis of Russian assistance to the Spanish Republic, see Cattell, *op. cit.,* Ch. 8.

134. Cf. Puzzo, *op. cit.,* pp. 147–48.

135. *Ibid.,* p. 212.

136. *Ibid.,* p. 93.

137. *Op. cit.,* p. 248.

138. Puzzo, *op. cit.,* pp. 151 f.

139. *Ibid.,* pp. 154–55 and n. 27.

140. For some references, see Allen Guttmann, *The Wound in the Heart: America and the Spanish Civil War* (New York, The Free Press, 1962), pp. 137–38. The earliest quasi-official reference that I know of is in Herbert Feis, *The Spanish Story* (New York, Alfred A. Knopf, 1948), where data is given in an appendix. Jackson (*op. cit.,* p. 256) refers to this matter, without noting that Texaco was violating a prior agreement with the Republic. He states that the American government could do nothing about this, since "oil was not considered a war material under the Neutrality Act." He does not point out, however, that Robert Cuse, the Martin Company, and the Mexican government were put under heavy pressure to withhold supplies from the Republic, although this too was quite legal. As noted, the Texaco Company was never even branded "unethical" or "unpatriotic," these epithets of Roosevelt's being reserved for those who tried to assist the Republic. The cynic might ask just why oil was excluded from the Neutrality Act of January 1937, noting that while Germany and Italy were capable of supplying arms to Franco, they could not meet his demands for oil.

The Texaco Oil Company continued to act upon the pro-Nazi sympathies of its head, Captain Thorkild Rieber, until August 1940, when the publicity began to be a threat to business. See Feis, *op. cit.,* for further details. For more on these matters, see Richard P. Traina, *American Diplomacy and the Spanish Civil War* (Bloomington, Indiana University Press, 1968), pp. 166 f.

141. Puzzo, *op. cit.,* p. 160. He remarks: "A government in Madrid in which Socialists, Communists, and anarchists sat was not without menace to American business interests both in Spain and Latin America" (p. 165). Hull, incidentally, was in error about the acts of the Spanish government. The irresponsible

left-wing elements had not been given arms but had seized them, thus preventing an immediate Franco victory.

142. See Jackson, *op. cit.*, p. 458.

143. Cf. Guttmann, *op. cit.*, p. 197. Of course, American liberalism was always pro-
loyalist, and opposed both to Franco and to the revolution. The attitude towards the latter is indicated with accuracy by this comparison, noted by
Guttmann, p. 165: "300 people met in Union Square to hear Liston Oak [see
note 123] expose the Stalinists' role in Spain; 20,000 met in Madison Square
Garden to help Earl Browder and Norman Thomas celebrate the preservation of bourgeois democracy," in July 1937.

144. *Ibid.*, p. 198.

145. To conclude these observations about the international reaction, it should be
noted that the Vatican recognized the Franco government *de facto* in August
1937 and *de jure* in May 1938. Immediately upon Franco's final victory, Pope
Pius XII made the following statement: "Peace and victory have been willed
by God to Spain . . . which has now given to proselytes of the materialistic
atheism of our age the highest proof that above all things stands the eternal
value of religion and of the Spirit." Of course, the position of the Catholic
Church has since undergone important shifts—something that cannot be said
of the American government.

146. See note 60.

147. See, for example, the reference to Machajski in Harold D. Lasswell, *The
World Revolution of Our Time: A Framework for Basic Policy Research* (Hoover Institute Studies; Stanford, Calif., Stanford University Press, 1951); reprinted,
with extensions, in Harold D. Lasswell and Daniel Lerner, eds., *World Revolutionary Elites: Studies in Coercive Ideological Movements* (Cambridge, Mass., The
M.I.T. Press, 1965), pp. 29–96. Daniel Bell has a more extensive discussion of
Machajski's critique of socialism as the ideology of a new system of exploitation in which the "intellectual workers" will dominate, in a very informative
essay that bears directly on a number of the topics that have been mentioned
here: "Two Roads from Marx: The Themes of Alienation and Exploitation,
and Workers' Control in Socialist Thought," in *The End of Ideology*, pp.
335–68.

148. Lasswell, *op. cit.*, p. 85. In this respect, Lasswell's prognosis resembles that of
Bell in the essays cited earlier.

149. Summarized in the *Christian Science Monitor*, March 15, 1968. I have not seen
the text and therefore cannot judge the accuracy of the report.

150. To mention just the most recent example: on January 22, 1968, McNamara testified before the Senate Armed Services Committee that "the evidence appears overwhelming that beginning in 1966 Communist local and guerrilla forces have sustained substantial attrition. As a result, there has been a drop in combat efficiency and morale. . . ." The Tet offensive was launched within a week of this testimony. See *I. F. Stone's Weekly,* February 19, 1968, for some highly appropriate commentary.

151. The reality behind the rhetoric has been amply reported. A particularly revealing description is given by Katsuichi Honda, a reporter for *Asahi Shimbun,* in *Vietnam—A Voice from the Villages,* 1967, obtainable from the Committee for the English Publication of "Vietnam—a Voice from the Villages," c/o Mrs. Reiko Ishida, 2-13-7, Nishikata, Bunkyo-Ku, Tokyo.

11/23